Praise for *The Wondrous Toy Workshop*

"Hanni Sager is an example of the best in humanity: she helps, she supports; her will to create is demonstrable and contagious; her integrity is unquestionable; her imagination and sensitivity are manifested in what she makes. Her creativity knows no bounds, and what she sees and touches she transforms.

Hanni's living now in her paradise on the Calle de los Ensueños, in San Agustín Etla, Oaxaca. There we see her garden, her wooden birds, her caterpillar made of tin cans, and her altar to Frida Kahlo, who must be watching and admiring Hanni from above—all of her, her iron will, her creativity, her playfulness like that of a young girl.

Hanni, we continue to enrich ourselves through your spirit. May the festival of your imagination and sensitivity never stop!"

—*Edmundo Aquino, painter, sculptor, printmaker*

"Hanni is a monarch, a monarch butterfly fleeing the Canadian cold and arriving in a Mexican sanctuary, seeking the warmth of these lands and these skies. Her wings are beautiful. She recognizes no limits or frontiers. Hanni, our monarch, teaches us by her example and generous spirit."

—*Othón Cuevas, Director, Centéotl Community Development Project and Federal Congressman, Mexico*

"At a time when parents are concerned about contaminated toys coming from China, it's nice to see a book that shows us how to have fun making our own: *The Wondrous Toy Workshop* reminds us of the pleasure we can take in our own creations. It also shows us a clear alternative to children doing dangerous work on the street."

—*David L. Parker, author of* Before Their Time: The World of Child Labor

"Masterfully told by Nancy Miller, this is the story of Hanni Sager, a disabled maker, collector, and lover of toys, who, in one of the poorest places in the Americas, finds a group of disabled children. Hanni teaches them to construct toys and thus makes them understand that as human beings, no matter what their disability, they can transcend their condition, help themselves, even others, and in the process achieve dignity and appreciation of their own worth and creativity. Toys are the means whereby throughout our lives we are all able to create, love, and be free—the most valuable forces urging us on to overcome the many obstacles we find in our way.

The toys designed by Hanni Sager are based on the cultural traditions of the children who made them. I have yet to find anyone not tempted to play with these beautiful objects when they touch them, a true sign of Hanni Sager's—and the children's—indomitable spirit."

—*Susana Wald, author of* Spanish for Dummies

The Wondrous Toy Workshop

The Wondrous Toy Workshop

*Hanni's Inspiring Life
and Her Toys That Anyone Can Make*

Nancy B. Miller

*For David —
We're so glad to
have you in our
midst!*

Nancy

SYREN BOOK COMPANY
MINNEAPOLIS

Published by
Syren Book Company
5120 Cedar Lake Road
Minneapolis, MN 55416
763-398-0030
www.syrenbooks.com

Printed in the United States of America on acid-free paper

ISBN-13: 978-0-929636-82-5

LCCN 2007939038

Photographs of toys and Hanni Sager by Lynda Wilde
Photographs of children by Centéotl, Piña Palmera,
and David Werner for PROJIMO
Author photograph by Cynthia Stokes
Cover photograph © David Werner for PROJIMO
Cover design by Kyle G. Hunter
Interior text design by Wendy Holdman

To order additional copies of this book please go to www.itascabooks.com

A portion of the proceeds from sale of this book will be donated to the Fondo de Becas (Scholarship Fund) of the Casa de la Mujer (Women's House) in Oaxaca, Mexico. Scholarships go to well-qualified young indigenous women who would not be able to complete their high school education without the financial help and mentoring these scholarships provide. Donations (tax-deductible in the United States) are always welcome. They may be sent to the Casa de la Mujer, 3a Privada de Guadalupe Victoria No. 107, Colonia Libertad, Oaxaca, Oax. 68090, Mexico.

Information about PROJIMO, a nonprofit Community-Based Rehabilitation program, and allied programs can be found at www.healthwrights.org.

For Hanni, who made it all happen

Contents

Foreword

The Wondrous Toy Workshop is a practical how-to-do-it book about making toys. It is also an inspiring story about helping disadvantaged children build worthwhile lives for themselves, realize their creative potential, and gain self-esteem.

The heroine of this mesmerizing story by Nancy Miller is a down-to-earth older woman named Hanni Sager, who herself has a physical disability. Perhaps because of her own impairment, Hanni developed a remarkable understanding of human nature and human needs, along with a deep empathy for young people in difficult circumstances. Hanni grew up in Switzerland, migrated to Canada, and in later life ended up in southern Mexico. On the west coast of Oaxaca, in a Community-Based Rehabilitation (CBR) program for disabled children called Piña Palmera, she found a new calling: toy making with disabled children and eventually with street children.

I first learned of Hanni's toys long before I learned of Hanni. For years I'd been involved with another CBR program, named PROJIMO, 700 miles to the north, in the state of Sinaloa. When a group of us from PROJIMO visited Piña Palmera, we saw the eagerness and artistic creativity with which the youngsters there were making playful, stimulating toys. We took back samples and set about making similar playthings with disabled children together with schoolchildren, in PROJIMO's own "Children's Toy-Making Workshop." Everyone, young and old, loved the way the imaginatively painted animals and birds, cowboys and señoritas, flapped their wings or did somersaults. It was hard to say which was more fun, making the toys or playing with them.

The Wondrous Toy Workshop provides simple, clear instructions—complete with helpful line drawings—on how to create a menagerie of popular toys. Both the toys and the children making them are brought to life in a kaleidoscope of colorful photos.

But equally moving is Hanni's own story, which is beautifully told by her friend Nancy Miller, who lovingly portrays the way Hanni learned to help the children discover their creative potential and how Hanni herself grew in the process. Hanni's refreshing insight into the psychology of vulnerable children comes not from an academic background but from opening up her heart to the children and encouraging them to do the same with her and with each other.

Having started with disabled children in rural areas, Hanni went on to work with urban street children. Despite their physical limitations, she found disabled children easier to work with because they were so happy to learn from someone who focused on their strengths, not their weaknesses. The street kids, by contrast, tended to be more unruly and less trusting of well-meaning adults. They were quick and full of energy but showed little patience. With such children, Hanni discovered, you need to teach them by using physical things.

"This is the opposite," Hanni explains, "of how you work with disabled kids, who always think because they can't run. With street kids, it's mostly grab and run—how fast can they get it? They have to unlearn that way of working, to see that there is something of value in slowness." Hanni has been able to adapt her teaching methods to a wide range of children because she respects each child and challenges each child to do the best he or she can.

The beauty of Nancy Miller's book—apart from the simple charm of the toys themselves—is the spectrum of stories she tells about the sundry children involved. Although the focus is on making toys, the empowering approach to working with disabled and marginalized children makes *The Wondrous Toy Workshop* a groundbreaking contribution to the pedagogy of the disadvantaged.

—David Werner

David Werner, writer and health activist, is the author of *Where There Is No Doctor*, a manual for health promoters now in 90 languages around the world. He has been a consultant to UNICEF, WHO, UNDP, UN-ESCAP, the Peace Corps, and the World Bank and has received numerous fellowships and awards.

Introductory Note

The story I'm about to tell you struck me as one of universal importance, one that insisted on being documented so that it could be used as a guide by others whose generosity of spirit is the equal of Hanni Sager's.

This book has two parts. The first is the story of a life whose purpose has emerged with shining clarity—an enviable state of affairs in a world where daunting complexity, not-so-far-off dangers, and competing responsibilities and desires often make us feel we're swimming in a hazardous, murky soup. In this part of the book you'll find, in Hanni's own lively language, stories of some of the children whose lives she has touched with such remarkable effect.

The second part of the book is a simple, straightforward handbook for setting up a toy-making workshop like the ones Hanni established in the southeastern Mexican state of Oaxaca. The physical requirements are minimal and the potential rewards are enormous. This book is intended as well for parents and others who—with or without their children, establishing a workshop or not—just want to have fun making toys.

The patterns for Hanni's toys, which appear at the end of the book, are in the public domain and she hopes they will be used as widely as possible.

Although the central figures in the book are children, the principles involved are applicable to adults as well as to children, for there are both children and adults everywhere in the world who need validation of their humanity and inherent creativity.

Read on, and be inspired!

Acknowledgments

First, my profound thanks to David Werner, who, with his early understanding of what this book is about and his warm encouragement, let me know that it was worth pursuing. To Lynda Wilde, a dear friend who never complained about multiple re-dos, for her beautiful photos of the toys that enliven this book. To my esteemed friend Susana Wald, who brings excellence to every project she touches, in this case editing, advising, and making helpful connections for me. To the sainted Jim Little for leading me with unflagging patience through questions with my computer. To Cheryl Seim and Roberta Christie for being faithful couriers between Hanni in Mexico and me in Minneapolis. To so many other friends who made thoughtful suggestions and gave me support throughout, among them Carol Anderson, Lane Ayres, Jim Charlton, Barry Head, Peter McCallion, Marion McNurlen, and Arnold Walker. To my superb team at Syren and, oh, yes, to my friends at Kinko's in downtown Minneapolis, who with their brains and their humor, were always there to give me help when I needed it.

Hanni Sager, the Wonder Worker

Hanni Sager was born in 1938 in the hills of Switzerland, south of Zurich, where she spent a happy childhood playing with eleven sisters and brothers. Then, after finishing college as a fashion designer, she emigrated to Canada. It was there she heard, for the first time, a child saying, "I'm  bored!" "Turn off the TV and start playing!" she said, but the child had no idea what she meant. Then and there, Hanni says, she knew that Canada was missing something and she started looking for toys truly native to Canada, but she found little more than hockey pucks.

During the 1980s, while she lived in Toronto, Hanni organized large and immensely popular toy exhibitions and toy workshops at Toronto's cultural center Harbourfront. She gave talks about toys and antique dolls and became well known as Toronto's Toy Lady. In 1993, she curated the exhibition "The Art of Playing" at the Hamilton Art Gallery, in Hamilton, Ontario, another popular event that confirmed her belief that *everyone* likes to play.

When she began to spend time in Mexico, Hanni discovered the richness of handmade, traditional toys. She loved sitting in the park, watching children happily play with these simple toys—this was *playing*.

Disabled herself, Hanni wanted to work with disabled children, so in 1991 she went to Piña Palmera, a center for disabled children in Zipolite, a small coastal town in Oaxaca, in southeastern Mexico. There she established the first of what were to become four toy-making workshops in Oaxaca, bringing not only joy to the children—and to the adults around them as well—but a new sense of their self-worth as valuable, creative human beings.

Back in Canada, in 1995, Hanni was recognized with a medal for her work there with disabled children and adults, and in 2001, she was awarded

Canada's prestigious Medal for Meritorious Service for teaching both children and adults how to make toys. But medals can't compete with the rewards she gets from seeing the smiles on children's faces as they complete their first toy that works. "The impossible is made possible!" she says.

Now Hanni makes her home in a small house she designed to accommodate her disability, in the beautiful hills of Oaxaca. She has built a toy workshop there, where she's now teaching teachers how to make toys and where she plans to invite small groups of children to toy-making fun as well. With all this life-giving activity and supervising a growing Stone Garden, she hardly has time, she says, to watch the hummingbirds in the bougainvillea.

The Wondrous Toy Workshop

Chapter 1

How It Began

Working with Disabled Children

Tino's Story

Then there's Tino, who was born with muscular dystrophy. They die very young, you know. Hopefully, he could live until he was twenty-five, but he was very disabled, spending all his waking hours in a wheelchair. The only strength he had was in his left hand and he could turn that only a quarter of a circle.

Even the director of the center said he was too disabled to produce anything, but I said, "No, I'm here for him." His mother and I got him set up with a little table on his wheelchair, all the colors he wanted, water for mixing the paints, and he started to paint. I remember thinking during the first week, "I can't stand this" because we had to watch every move he made. But little by little, he began to paint, with us sitting there beside him. It wasn't long before he began to paint exquisitely—postcards—and then he began to sell them! This is why I say nothing is impossible. It is possible!

—Hanni Sager

Who is this woman with her profound belief in limitless possibility? What led her to become a modern-day miracle worker? And where did the miracle of Tino take place, with consequences reaching far beyond the center where Tino and the woman first met?

Hanni Sager knows a lot about disability, pain, and the deep despair that disability can bring: she's had muscular dystrophy for many years. Muscular dystrophy is a fairly rare disease that affects primarily the voluntary muscles and often makes movement difficult and painful. Her fundamental joy, however, has been made visible in her remarkable collection of toys from around the world and other evidences of her core belief that no one is fully human without knowing how to play.

Swiss-born and -raised, Hanni is a Canadian citizen. In Toronto, she became well known for the enormously popular Christmas events involving toys and play that she put on for ten years at Toronto's great cultural center, Harbourfront. She became known as Toronto's Toy Lady.

When Hanni's illness seemed almost more than she could bear, the gift of an airline ticket to Mexico from a loving friend and a place to stay in San Miguel de Allende with another friend served as her introduction to Mexico and brought her renewed appetite for life.

Hanni continued to go back to Mexico every winter, usually just short visits to San Miguel. Later, in the 1980s, on a brief trip to the Maya country in the Mexican state of Chiapas, she passed through the neighboring state of Oaxaca (wah-HAH-kah). She fell in love with the capital city of that name and decided this was her kind of place. A Spanish colonial city, Oaxaca has beautiful architecture and a strong indigenous character, full of warmth and hospitality. She now lives in the nearby countryside in a house she designed to accommodate her disability.

Hanni was enchanted by the traditional toys she saw in Mexico. They were simple, beautiful, and often funny. But in the early 1980s, mass-produced plastic toys were beginning to appear. Children were beginning to gravitate toward them and to reject the less-than-slick traditional toys their fathers made for them. "That really scared me," Hanni says. "It was a whole epoch, a whole civilization dwindling away." So she began to collect these toys and took them back to Toronto, where she exhibited and gave talks about them.

Hanni especially loved the toys associated with Mexico's Day of the Dead, celebrated in early November. This is an occasion on which Mexicans honor their dead by building altars that feature the departed's favorite food and drink and other memorabilia; some people share picnics with them in the cemetery. Replicas of skeletons abound in every size, humorously acting out the lives of their fleshier counterparts. Miniature skeletons pop up when the lid of a tiny coffin is slid back. Sugar-candy skulls, bright with shiny paper and colored-frosting decorations, bear the names of those to whom they are given as gifts. These toys were of particular interest to Hanni because so many of us regard death as a taboo topic, let alone as an integral part of daily life. As the joke has it, some of us like to think of death as optional.

Tino's miracle took place at Piña Palmera, a center for disabled children—a rarity then in Mexico—on Oaxaca's beautiful Pacific coast, near the tourist towns of Zipolite and Puerto Escondido. Hanni had found her way there as a volunteer, hoping to interest the children in creative work with fabrics and thread, something she is very good at.

At the time of Hanni's first visit to Piña Palmera, the center was just a cluster of a few simple structures nestled in a grove of tall, graceful coconut palms. The sides of most of these shelters were open to the warm air of the sea just a few hundred yards away. Palm-thatch roofs were all that gave protection from the heavy rains that come each summer. Later, everything but the center's one cement-block building, a dormitory, was swept away by Hurricane Pauline. As though to emphasize her irresistible force, Nature not long afterwards inflicted a second hurricane, Rick, on the Oaxaca coast, destroying what existed of Piña Palmera's newly sprouting structures. Miraculously, the staff was able to get the children to safety in both storms and no one was hurt. Ultimately, a more resilient Piña Palmera rose out of what first appeared to be hopeless debris.

It was lucky that on her first visit to Piña Palmera, in 1990, Hanni took with her some of the traditional Mexican toys that had so intrigued her in San Miguel, for the children at the center simply weren't interested in the fabrics and threads she had brought with her. They did, however, make bags to keep their clothes in, and now they had something clean to put their heads on when they went to bed on their straw mats on the floor.

When Hanni learned that the man who ran the center's modestly equipped carpentry shop was to be away for a couple of months, she thought,

"This is the time to make some traditional toys." All the toys Hanni had brought with her and wanted to reproduce were simple toys that could be made from plywood with parts that moved by pulling strings. She took the toys apart, traced the individual pieces as patterns, and learned how to work with a power scroll saw. "I'm petrified of the saw," she says, "but when these incredible disabled kids eventually got over their shyness about participating, they'd get right on the saw without a twinge. It was so frightening, I could hardly stand to watch."

It wasn't easy at first to get the children to work with her. They merely stood around the edges and observed. "For days, I worked by myself, with all those pairs of eyes around me clearly thinking, 'She's the artist, not us. Will she give up?' I'd say, 'Anybody can do it. I never made a toy in my life, and if I can do it with these crippled hands, you can do it, too.' They didn't believe it, of course, and made fun of me. And the more they made fun, the more I insisted on everybody's being there at ten in the morning to watch me work. We'd have lunch together, then go back to the workshop until four, when they would leave."

Then, on a day when Hanni was unable to handle the drill to make the necessary holes in a toy bird's wing, Lider, a boy with one arm, said, "I'll help you." "My gosh, what a pair we'll be!" thought Hanni. But Lider took the drill and made the holes where Hanni—quaking with the thought of what might happen—told him to.

"Would you like to start making a toy?" Hanni asked him. "Oh, I don't think I can," he replied. "Look," she said, "what you do is put the pattern on a piece of wood and you trace it . . . ," and the boy with one arm, to his astonishment, became a toy maker.

Little by little, when the other children saw what fun Lider and Hanni were having and how proud they were of their accomplishment, they too began to participate. "I knew," Hanni says, "that if I got one kid, just one kid, I had them all. Before you knew it, more kids came in and we were all having fun. In fact, it was really funny: when we got to painting the toys, the mothers and the other adults around the center all wanted to join in and paint, too. The joke was that nobody would be in the kitchen or the office because they were all in my workshop."

Carlos's Story

Carlos was a young man of twenty-five when I met him. He's blind, and for eight years all he'd done was just walk around with a radio turned on. One day I asked him to come to the workshop. I showed him how to sand the toy parts and to put on the primer coat of paint—he could do that. It was marvelous! Every day, he was the first one to show up—he wanted to work. He couldn't see, he'll never see, but he could feel the pieces. Then I heard him talking to other people about "when we made the toys" and now he was a part of "we." Once you give them that dignity, that's where the reward is. That's the pay you get, when these so-called vegetables, blind or on the ground and doing nothing for years and years, can say, "I am a part of this."

—H. S.

At the beginning, there were practically no materials to work with at Piña Palmera, for it was a shoestring operation. Paintbrushes were a case in point. The center boasted perhaps seven or eight limp, wispy brushes that were too thin to carry paint, and there was no money to buy new ones. In a supreme instance of ingenuity, after trying to paint with fingers and rags, Hanni and the children began to experiment with the other materials about them. There were plenty of palm branches and bamboo around to serve as paintbrush handles, but what to use for bristles? They began with their own hair, but it proved too soft to be manageable. After more experimentation, the most successful bristles turned out to come from the hair of a few more or less willing dogs. Happily, a cry for help from Hanni to her family in Switzerland brought a whole box of paintbrushes and other supplies, but in the meantime a great lesson in resourcefulness had been learned by everyone.

One day, Hanni realized that all the toys they made consisted of male figures. "The acrobat was a man, the boxer was a man, everything was male. I thought, 'There's something really wrong here and we're going to have to change it. We're out of balance, we have to get women in here.' So I designed a woman, Mara the Acrobat, and I made her really sexy and gorgeous. I remember I was so excited when I made her and she really flipped over. The kids just laughed at me and said, 'She's crazy!' But it's very interesting: now they have four acrobat designs to choose from, and they almost always choose to make the woman.

"I'd say to the boys, 'You men, you think you're so terrific, but without a woman you're nothing!' It's the same with guns. I don't make anything with guns. I put a bunch of flowers in their hands. I explain to the kids that we don't need any more guns and they understand. But I leave it up to them. If they want to put guns in their toys' hands, they can. But I have yet to see a kid who does. It shows me that we're influencing these children, we're communicating with them, and they have a choice. I would never tell them what to do—I tell them why I'm doing what I do, why I think it's necessary."

Hanni's good at letting people do things their own way. Some of this she learned from an old Scot she had met in Australia. He had established a weaving workshop for Aborigine craftspeople, superb artists, and their weavings sold extremely well. However, it was impossible to take orders because of the Aborigines' tradition of the Walk About—simply departing for a month or two or maybe more. "There's no point in being frustrated or angry," the old man said. "This is their country and their way of life," and he adapted his life to theirs.

The children at Piña Palmera grew increasingly involved in the toy workshop and became enthusiastic toy makers. It wasn't all easy, however. They made mistakes—painting two left wings for the bird, for example, or making errors in measuring that prevented a toy's working properly. Hanni developed a system that gave increasing responsibility to each child. First, she demonstrated how to make a toy, explaining each step as she went. Then she set the children to making the toy themselves, providing help where she saw it was needed. With the third step, each child was on his or her own—free to make mistakes and to correct them. Left wings did get painted at first, but that and other mistakes were rarely repeated.

Hanni's methods produced many side benefits. The children learned, for instance, the importance of arithmetic and how to measure. They learned how to behave responsibly in the workshop. Every child had a small box in which to keep paintbrushes and toys in process: if brushes weren't properly washed at the end of each session, the consequence was having to paint with a gummed-up brush the next time.

Isaías and Élida's Story

Sometimes there was another kind of help I could give the kids. There was Isaías, for example. He was a handsome, wonderful boy of about ten when I first met him. He'd had polio and was always in a wheelchair—never expected to get out of it. He was so quick at learning how to make the toys that they used to call him "Hanni." A girl named Élida was also in a wheelchair from polio and she was smart, too. They came to the workshop every day, and we became very good friends.

Ana, the center's director, told me, "The kids look at you and talk about you all the time. They've never seen a disabled person as old as you walking around with braces." I guess I looked like their grandmother!

Then the therapist said to me, "It would be so great if you'd show the older kids how you exercise. They think it's a waste of time, and they never see disabled people older than twenty or twenty-five."

So we set the day, put mats on the floor, and got everybody out of their wheelchairs. Each one had a therapist to help and I showed them the whole routine I'd had to do for the past thirty-five years. It's not very exciting—it's boring—but I really believe you have to do it.

A week or two later, Isaías was waiting for me at the gate—on crutches. I looked at him and said, "Isaías, do you know how handsome you are? You're so tall, you're so handsome!" I couldn't believe it—he was actually walking on crutches. "You know, Hanni," he said, "I want to learn everything you're going to tell me, and I'm never going to be in a wheelchair ever again!"

I had such a weak spot for him, I had to be careful not to show the other kids. He was so bright and wonderful, never a problem, and he was such a good example to all the other children. Now they know what they have to do, and they accept it. When Isaías went to school, he'd walk on his crutches more than a kilometer every day.

The last I heard, Élida was running the little library there at the center, such a good organizer, and I think she and Isaías became novios, *sweethearts. This is what I was dreaming of six years before—what they could do if they just had the chance.*

—H. S.

Many children still had the idea that each new toy Hanni introduced would be too complicated for them to make. "Oh, I could never make that" was often heard. But Hanni would say, "Okay, we'll talk about that in another month" and then continue to nudge and encourage with a sure instinct for just how hard to push, given each child's individual disability and innate capacity. When a child began work on a new toy, she'd note the date. Then, when the toy was successfully completed, she would photograph it and give proof of accomplishment to the delighted child.

As Hanni often says, it wasn't just the children who learned from these experiences. She, too, grew in enlarged understanding. A poignant example occurred in Toronto, in Paul Hogan's inspired Spiral Garden for children at the Hugh Macmillan Rehabilitation Centre. Paul Hogan's projects for children always start with seeds and the idea of growth, although they may include such things as statues and "dream houses" built by the children from junk. Everybody learns to plant, to nurture their crops, to reap their harvests—and then feast on what they grew. At the invitation of a children's hospital in Sri Lanka, Hogan began a Butterfly Garden there. To start the garden, he took with him a small boat woven by the Toronto children from twigs and vines and filled with seeds from their own Spiral Garden.

At Hogan's invitation, Hanni designed for the Toronto Spiral Garden a giant, sixteen-foot-tall version of her bird with the flapping wings as a source of exercise for the young patients. To pull the ropes that raised the wings became an activity vied for among the youngsters, who hated taking the exercise the doctors prescribed for them.

While the bird, a big, black crow, was under construction, all the children were invited to sew some shiny ornament to the fabric that covered the wings. But there was a rule: each child had to do the sewing without help. When a girl of twelve came to Hanni and said she wanted to be included, Hanni, seeing that the child had no arms but only little hands that emerged from her shoulders, told her with deep regret about the rule. "Why do you think I can't do that?" the girl asked—and proceeded to flex her shoulders, thread the needle, and sew on her own ornament. Born without arms, the girl had been encouraged by her mother from her earliest years to think of herself as a capable, fully functioning human being. With this stunning incident, Hanni learned that you can never underestimate anyone's capacity and will.

After a few months at Piña Palmera, Hanni's children had produced enough creditable, workable toys so that they now had something to show their parents and other adults working around the treatment center. They spread their toys out on a long table in the simple shack that was their workshop, put modest prices on them, and invited everyone to come for an open house. It was a huge success. The parents were bursting with pride and nearly every toy was sold. Suddenly this became another area for responsible growth and maturing.

While Hanni's first—and always first—intention was to give a sense of self-worth to each child and to encourage the creativity she passionately believes resides in every one of us, it was now clear that the toys might represent a source of some small income to their makers. A few pesos in the pockets of children who mostly came from impoverished backgrounds could mean the independence to buy a piece of candy, or even to contribute to the family's slender financial resources.

But quality toys didn't come about overnight. Making good toys isn't always easy, and when toys were sloppily painted or didn't move as they were intended to, the tourists the children approached on the beach wouldn't buy them. Hanni says, "I would hold up a toy and say to the children, 'Would you want to buy that? Who wants to pay for something like that?' At times the kids got discouraged and wouldn't make any toys at all, but if you don't sand the toy and paint it well, you just don't get the money." So some abandoned the project, but they almost always came back. And for what? For the fun of making a toy and doing it well, Hanni believes. "There's something so rewarding about doing a job well, and that goes on throughout your life."

There were other things for everyone to learn as well. For one, there had to be organization: it was necessary to keep track of what was made and who sold it and for how much, all lessons in the importance of numbers and the usefulness of bookkeeping. It would be good, too, Hanni felt, for the children to assume responsibility for a small part of the cost of materials. So they paid just a few pesos to the workshop for each toy they sold and got to keep the rest.

Eventually, the children individually got to decide whether to sell their toys directly themselves, on the beach; to employ a middle person, if necessary, who got a percentage of the sale price; or to send their toys with those of others to shops in Puerto Escondido or the city of Oaxaca. Not surprisingly, quality went up as the children saw what would sell and what would not. After treatment with medication and physiotherapy or recovery from operations, young patients would return to their villages. Two of these were Chico and Tilo, who had come down to Piña Palmera from their home in the small community of San Mateo Piña, high in the mountains above Zipolite. "Tilo had club feet and couldn't speak properly," Hanni recalls, "but he was such a fast learner, and so was Chico. When they went back, we thought what a great idea it would be if they could have a workshop up there where they could keep on making toys and maybe get other disabled kids involved, too."

Hanni was quite right. Several adults on the Piña Palmera staff whom she had taught to make toys and who had caught her excitement and pleasure in making them, went up to San Mateo Piña and a new enterprise was born. Again, involvement of the adults of the community gave support to the workshop, and when the children had produced enough toys for a show, a special occasion was planned to honor Hanni for her work.

But Hanni was unable to make the trip. In 1992, during a visit to San Miguel, she was in a bad automobile accident that almost ended her inspiring work—and her life. For a week she lay in a coma, her already damaged body even more mangled now. Surgery was needed to restore an eye to its proper position, and when she first looked at herself in a mirror after the bandages came off, she was horrified. She lay in bed in the house of friends for six weeks, once again thinking that life was too much to bear.

One day, the friends' housekeeper, a warm and loving woman who cared for Hanni, kept her clean, and gave her daily massage, said to her, "You know, we Nahuas believe that everyone gets two lives—the second to finish up the work we didn't complete in the first one." It was enough to give Hanni the courage to go on.

The following year, when she was again invited to San Mateo Piña, the trip seemed doubtful at first. The single-lane, rutted road was more of a burro trail in those days, its bridges regularly washed out by the summer rains. It would be a difficult journey for any traveler but a particularly arduous one for Hanni. Nevertheless, she made the effort, and what an event it was.

Everyone came out to see the children's work displayed, and the mayor of the village made a speech of thanks to Hanni. Hanni responded in her fractured Spanish, but what she said was clear to everyone: "I'm here because I am part of you, and it is the toys that have connected us. And where I am, in Canada or Switzerland or anywhere else, you are now a part of me and the world out there."

Then the mayor said a startling thing: "Until the workshop came up here, I didn't know we had so many disabled children living among us." As in so many communities, not just in Mexico but around the world, "defective" children are frequently hidden away and unacknowledged. It was a revelation to him and to others.

Hanni delightedly promised to return again despite the difficulty of the trip, but with one parting shot to the mayor: "I've seen those bags of cement you've got lying around here. I'll come back when you've made ramps so that your kids can go to the toilet when they want to, without having to ask for help. You don't know how a little ramp can make such a difference in somebody's life and let someone be proud of what he can do alone."

Hanni joked with the mayor: "These kids will probably make more money with their toys than their parents do raising coffee beans. When they can buy a helicopter to carry me, I'll be back!"

For Hanni, the great reward is, and always has been, uncovering the rich potential she knows lies beneath a damaged surface. She loves integrating disabled people with people who are not disabled, for, as she says, "You can learn such a lot from disabled people, how they function, how incredibly tolerant and patient they can be. None of us is a perfect Barbie doll—that's not humanity! I want to give people the awareness that they are real, valid human beings. That's the most we can do for anybody.

"Sometimes I think I was just in the right place at the right time, at the right age. Thirty-five years earlier, before the relapse of my dystrophy, I couldn't have done what I've done. I was a businesswoman, I had a shop, I was in a marriage, and I was a conformist. I probably had to go through all this to come out at the other end, to be sort of hit on the head and to realize that my former life wasn't all that good and that it was time to try something else. I just wish I had more stamina because I tire easily, working with disabled and mentally retarded kids. It's very hard work because you have to be concentrating all the time. But the rewards are so unbelievably high!"

Working with Street Children

While living in Oaxaca for several months each winter, Hanni stayed in an apartment next to that of Marieke Bekkers, a young Dutch anthropologist who had directed her to Piña Palmera. Marieke's goal was to start a center for the care of the street children who were the subject of her thesis. When she and Hanni dreamed about what the center would offer, Hanni would always say, "And I want a workshop in it."

When Hanni returned from Piña Palmera, she found that Marieke had raised a large amount of money from individuals and foundations in Holland to establish the center she'd hoped for. The center, located in the city of Oaxaca, provided some schooling and at least two meals a day to the thirty-five to fifty children who came there, but it didn't keep them overnight. The children ranged in age from four to about nineteen or twenty, most of the older ones with mental problems. The center later had a house in which seven or eight teenagers successfully lived together under supervision, going to school and learning how to care for themselves and their home.

When the center got up and running, Marieke said, "Now we write a proposal for the workshop." Together, she and Hanni constructed a proposal that provided money for the acquisition of equipment and materials needed for just the workshop that had been Hanni's dream.

But difficulties lay ahead. To begin with, street children are very different from disabled children. Most of them at the center in Oaxaca had one or two parents who were unable or unwilling to care for them. Many of them were simply on the loose from a very early age. Some were forced to work to supplement their family's meager income and most never saw the inside of a regular school. On their own, living by their wits, often the sexual prey of strangers, street children are frightened, distrustful of adults, always on the go, with survival their first concern. Unlike disabled children, for many of whom every movement requires concentration and patience, these children are often quarrelsome, disrespectful, and concentrate only with difficulty.

"These street kids are like schizophrenics, like really crazy kids. They can't sit still. If they don't like something they throw it away. They beat each other up. But if you get one or two making something, the others get curious and start to come in, little by little. They see a good thing and they want to be a part of it.

"I had one girl who would beat up all the others when she came in every morning. When I asked her why she did it, she said, 'I like to.' 'But it hurts,' I said. 'Well, I don't care—I want to do it.' 'Okay,' I said, 'today you're not going to do that. You sit beside me.' Slowly, the girl could see another outlet for her energy, a positive outlet. Sometimes, when the other kids weren't around, she'd even climb up on my lap and ask for hugs. Of course they are so negative because they've been kicked around and abused so much. I'm no psychiatrist, but I do understand what they have to go through every day just to survive.

"It was terribly hard at the children's center," Hanni says. "It took me about six weeks to get this bunch of twenty-five or more kids to sit down on chairs to draw a pattern or to paint. They would get up and sit down, get up and sit down. They'd run around with the paint and brushes in their hands, pushing each other around. It was a game, and it drove me crazy.

"They gave me some social workers and teachers who wanted to learn how to make toys and help out, but with kids like that you almost have to work one-on-one. You watch for a few months to see how capable a kid is, then you add another one, then another one. So I watched and observed and would go home utterly exhausted. I knew it wasn't working.

"One day, I went in and the place was a complete disaster. I couldn't believe that they would be so disorderly and disrespectful. I took a piece of wood, slammed it on the table, and said, 'That's it. I'm closing the shop. You don't respect it, you don't respect the machines, you don't respect the paint, you don't respect anything. There's no way we can work like that. If you don't want to make toys, get out there on the streets and prostitute yourselves and sell your rotten Chiclets.' I was just all-out livid.

"Then one of the social workers came to me and said, 'You can't talk to the children like this.' And I said, 'As for you, you're just decorations here. You won't even wash a kid's hair. I've told you from the beginning that it's not working. You're only babysitting these kids.

"They have no respect for you. They do what you tell them to do and then five minutes later they're laughing at you behind your back. I want small groups and I want to work with the most intelligent ones so that afterwards they can teach other kids. You can think about it. If you can't do that, then I'm not coming back. I'll give you two days to think about it. I'm going home.' I really let them have it.

"They couldn't believe it. When I came back a few days later, the director came to me and said, 'You know, we can't have one-on-one care because we don't have enough people. But you take the few kids you want and the others can go on with the social workers and we'll do it in smaller groups.' That started to work and it was so much easier, especially because I had a couple of smart and willing kids to work with who would soon pass their knowledge on to others."

It was around this time that Hanni took on the troubled boy called Remigio, a child of about nine. "He was very, very disturbed," Hanni says. "He couldn't be still a minute—I think he was abused—and every toy he painted was black or brown or gray. And he wouldn't make eyes on any of the animals. This told me something was severely wrong: he didn't want to see the world, he didn't want to know this world. I watched him and encouraged him and showed him, along with the other kids, how to make eyes: a drop of white, let it dry, then a drop of black. But he wouldn't do it.

"So one day I said, 'We're going to blindfold him.' We went for him and he screamed like murder and I said, 'Okay, tell us what you can see. You have no eyes, so what can you see?' He was wriggling and screaming and biting, and when we finally let him loose, he ran away. The whole staff really went after me: 'Now you've done it! He's never going to come back.' 'No,' I said, 'he'll come back in two or three days, and I'll bet you he's going to make eyes on the animals!'

"Well, he did come back two or three days later—and ignored me completely. I just worked with the few other kids and he came in again, watching me and coming closer and closer. I knew he wanted to work. 'You know, Remigio,' I said, 'I think you should just leave if you don't want to help. Why don't you bring all your animals here, all the things you've done, and we'll ask the other kids if they'll make eyes for them.' 'No,' he said, 'I want to make them.' I said, 'Great! Here's the white paint, I'll show you how to do it. Let's finish them and maybe we can sell them.' So then he finished them.

"Then I said, 'You know, I think you are really a magician. I think you are the magician of the color green.' 'Nobody can make green,' he said. 'No,' I said, 'I think you are the person who can make green. I'll give you yellow and I'll give you blue and I'll tell you what to do.' Then I gave him five drops of yellow and two drops of blue—I'll never forget it—and he started to mix them. It was incredible! When it turned into green, it was as though he was freaking out. It was like the best medicine I could have given him. Nothing could have worked better.

"When I said I didn't think it was enough to paint the whole bird and maybe we should mix some more, he really got into it. 'If you want green, I can make green now.' And everything he painted was green for about six weeks. I knew that I had brought him to a point where something was happening inside him—a kind of confidence that he was really somebody. I helped him make magenta and other colors and he came every day. He started to paint colors, to explore and to make things. Everybody, the whole staff could see the change in this kid and wanted to know what I did. I told them five drops of yellow and two drops of blue were the remedy."

Hanni's occasional tough treatment in dealing with the children was accompanied by a lot of low-level common sense, if there is such a thing. She had watched with scorn as the teachers gave blackboard lectures about how to grow plants, with no practical application in the center's neglected garden plot. "*Show* them!" Hanni thought. "I guess this is something else I have to do." So she bought a bag of sunflower seeds and told Remigio he was going to be in charge of the sunflowers. "I showed him a picture of what they were going to look like, and then we went into the garden and planted the seeds carefully, every two inches, and I explained how important the watering was. 'You're in charge of this plot now,' I told him. 'You're in charge of watering it and it's your garden. Nobody else is allowed in this garden. This garden is yours and it's your responsibility.'

"I think we started on a Wednesday and I couldn't be there on Friday, so he continued to watch and water and on Monday he saw the first little shoot come up. He ran to me, out of breath. 'Hanni, Hanni, Hanni!' It was so simple, but he'll never, never forget that. He brought a seed to become a plant. How much more can you want in life?"

Traditional classroom methods used with the street children had other shortcomings as well. When arithmetic was taught straight from books to these restless children who could hardly be kept at their desks, all the teachers got were blank looks and disruptive behavior. But when Hanni taught them with a toy that something had to be exactly seven centimeters, not eight, in order to work, they learned. Not quickly, but they learned. And when they got the hang of measuring, "Everything got measured," Hanni says, "arms, noses, everything!" and again they were having fun.

With children like this, Hanni declares, you need to teach by using physical things. "They only know physical energy, not brain energy. This is the opposite, of course, of how you work with disabled kids, who always think because they can't run. They're much easier for me to work with because they're so hungry for attention and really want to do something because they've been left sitting for so many years. Their enthusiasm is tremendous and they want to do things fast, but they can't because of their physical limitations. You have to say, 'No, you can't go so fast. Just learn to do one thing at a time and do it well.' Then they get there. With the street kids, it's mostly grab and run—how fast can they get it? They have to unlearn that way of working, to see that there is something of value hidden in slowness."

Sadly, Remigio's story doesn't have a happy ending. After Hanni returned to Canada, Remigio ran away from the center. The next—and last—time she saw him, he was once again washing windshields at stoplights. " 'Oh, my God, Remigio,' I said. 'Why aren't you at the center?' 'After you left, I left,' he said. 'If you come back, I'll come back.' There he was, only about eleven or twelve, cleaning windshields. I gave him all the change I had and that was it. I went home and cried and cried. You know, it breaks my heart. This was a human being who had potential. The worst of it was his loss of trust in people, in us. We were supposed to be there for him, and I left. I had to leave and go home. But somebody should have been there for him."

Hanni is highly critical of what can happen to organizations—everywhere in the world, not just in Mexico—when they become institutions. The caring idealism that was the inspiration for the center and other organizations like it begins to be obscured by, of all things, their success. Money comes in that permits the hiring of trained professionals—undoubtedly idealists themselves at one time—who have careers to think of. Administrative concerns, including the continued, preferably increased, funding of the organization loom ever larger as the organization grows and becomes more complex. The keeping of records and statistics on expensive equipment to justify the organization's existence somehow eclipses in importance the human needs they were meant to help meet. With layers of organization, hierarchies are inevitably established, not all of which work to the organization's benefit or that of the human beings they were meant to serve. In Hanni's view, this is what happened at the center.

An example took place there when Hanni, realizing the importance of involving as many of the children's families as possible, put on an open house at which the proud toy makers were hosts and could show off their accomplishments. Usually reluctant to come near the center where the "fancy" folks were in charge, but curious, even more parents, aunts, and uncles than anticipated accepted the invitation. The children's families were astonished by the imagination and charm of the toys their children had produced and talked enthusiastically together: *"My daughter made this!"* "See what my *son* did!"

Not only were the parents glowing with pride, some even said, "Maybe I could make a toy like that, too." Hanni says, "I knew they were dying to do it, too, because it's so normal to want to do something that's fun. I just wished I had the time to see what I could do in a year, integrating the families into the workshop."

Heartwarming as it was, the occasion was not repeated. "They never did it again," Hanni says. "I broke my brain trying to tell the staff how much the families want to be a part of it and how important it is to build up their trust, for them and others in the community to realize that the activity going on here is essential. And how it has to be done at their pace. So what if you put on an open house and only a few people show up the first time? They'll talk to others—curiosity again—and more will come the next time. You'll see.

"Furthermore, if a father or mother, an uncle or an aunt needs a job and is capable, he or she should be hired—even at half the salary of one of the teachers or social workers if the organization doesn't want to pay the whole thing. Give that person the responsibility for opening up these kids—they know their children better than anybody else. You don't need a degree. You just need a lot of patience, and many indigenous and less well-off or well-educated people have that. They've had to. So why not start with them? They can make mistakes and get frustrated, too, but give them a chance.

"I understand that we need to make jobs and to keep statistics," Hanni says, "but it's the statistics that have come to be our clients—not human beings."

Jorge's Story

Jorge was a boy of about fourteen, both legs disabled and with braces but a good-looking kid. A typical teenager, all he thought about was his hair, how gorgeous he looked, how great his five words of English were, how really tough and macho he was.

He wanted to come into the workshop, so I said, "Okay, this is how you start." "No," he said, "I don't want to start here, I want to do that." In ten minutes, he had the kids in an uproar. It was chaos in the workshop. He had this amazing power to get every kid on his side. The place was a mess, all because of Jorge. I thought, "You little rat, I'll show you," and I kicked him out.

When the director came and objected, I said, "I don't want him in this place. In ten minutes, he has the kids running around, throwing paint, doing stupid things." Jorge stayed outside then, but he'd call the kids out and together they'd shout and carry on and make fun of me.

For a while, he disappeared, went to stay with an aunt, I think, and I thought, "Great. A little peace and quiet now." But one day, he came back and said, "I'd really like to work." I said, "You? You want to work? You must be joking. What would you work at?" and he said, "I want to make the acrobat toy."

So I said, "Okay, this is how you start." I gave him the dirtiest work first, sanding, and I asked him how long he wanted to stay. "Fifteen minutes," he said. "Fine," I said. "Fifteen minutes. Start sanding here." He did, and in fifteen minutes I said, "All right, you can go now"—and thought to myself, "He'll never come back."

Well, he did. "How long are you going to work today?" I asked him. "Maybe twenty minutes," he said, and I gave him some really dirty work. When he'd worked about half an hour, I said, "Wow! You've worked ten minutes longer than you said you would. You can go now."

I think it was about the third or fourth day when he stayed and worked all day. I watched and watched him, and he was having fun, this conceited teenager! When the bell rang at two o'clock for comida, *the midday meal, I got up and said, "I think we should celebrate. Jorge worked four hours!" I made a big deal about this macho guy who'd worked four hours. The kids just laughed and I said, "I think maybe there's a chance for Jorge to do something worthwhile, not just think about girlfriends who leave him. Maybe there's a girlfriend who can see that he can do some really good work." I made him really important, and, you know, he turned out to be one of the best guys I ever had.*

—H. S.

Word of Hanni's successes at Piña Palmera and the center in Oaxaca quite naturally got around, and in 1995, she was invited to start a toy-making workshop in the newly established—and exceptionally well-run—community center at Zimatlán, a town about thirty kilometers outside the city of Oaxaca. This thriving center, Centéotl, run by a dedicated director, Othón Cuevas, has the enthusiastic support of its community. There people learn how to sew and cook, how to cut hair for money, and how to raise their own food in organic gardens. A tidy and growing library for young people was well used and tended, an especially important entity in a town that lost its public library because it didn't support the "right" candidates running for office under the flag of the party in power. A tiny museum at the center, cared for with enormous pride by the citizenry, housed pre-Columbian artifacts that had surfaced on their land.

Hanni's workshop at Zimatlán—with help from the Canadian embassy—involved not only children but their mothers as well. To sit at a table in the sun after school where some were cutting out toy parts and others were sanding or assembling or painting them and to listen to the companionable chatter that went on between the grown-ups and the children was sheer pleasure. Not only was everybody having a good time, but they, too, were now making toys in demand by the tourists in Oaxaca.

That wasn't always the case. Hanni worked at Zimatlán for four months, setting up the workshop and teaching the first few toys. At the end of the winter, with the workshop running nicely and in the hands of some capable adults, she returned to Toronto. When she came back the next winter, she learned that in her absence no one had made any of the toys she had taught; all they had produced were jigsaw puzzles with Batman and Smurfs on them.

"I was appalled," Hanni says, "and I asked them why they were doing that. One of the women said, 'Well, I'm a teacher and we got orders from the school to do educational toys, like jigsaw puzzles.' 'Who am I to tell them what they can or can't do?' I thought. 'How many did you sell?' I asked. 'None,' was the answer. 'So where are they?' 'In a box under the table'—and they were just garbage.

"I said, 'There's room for all of us in this world. Let's make this a year of experimenting. You see how many orders you can get, and I'll see how many orders we get for the toys I've been teaching.' Well, they didn't get any orders, but I came in one day with a big order for the traditional-style toys and I said, 'Now for the whole month we're going to do nothing but make these toys to fill the order, and even if we sell them at a very low price, we can get enough wood for at least three or four months' supply.' And we did.

"I think they really got it. What's the big deal, popping out 100,000 identical Barbies? To sit down and make one unique piece of art, that's what counts. I told them about how when I was asked to show some of these toys at a big toy convention in Switzerland the year before, people were crazy about them. I could have sold hundreds if I'd had them. People are hungry for something that's not mass produced." Another lesson learned.

The pleasure of the women and children in making toys with individuality (and its potential profitability) didn't go unnoticed by the women of Sola de Vega, a town south of Zimatlán. At their request, a bright and ambitious young woman named Zoila, an accomplished participant in the Zimatlán workshop who was studying to be an accountant, now went to Sola de Vega once a week. There she taught toy making to the women and children and how to run a profitable enterprise, the fifth Hanni-inspired workshop. Soon they, too, would send out their products for sale.

It's the qualities of enthusiasm, enduring patience, and the power to ob-serve that are needed by professionals and nonprofessionals wherever in the world there are disabled and disadvantaged people, children or adults. Happily, none of these traits requires a lot of education and advanced degrees.

"First," Hanni says, "you really have to like what you're doing and get a reward from it." And she's not talking about money. "If you get nothing out of it," Hanni says to volunteer helpers, "don't do it. It's not worth it, because you'll go home miserable. It should always be that first you get something out of it, then you can give back." (Hanni has outlived most muscular dystrophy sufferers, and in all likelihood it's because she is getting back the life she has given to so many.)

After enthusiasm for the job come patience and powers of observation, two qualities that are closely linked.

"First, you watch the individual, see what he can or can't do. Then you give him something he can do well—maybe it's sanding or maybe it's cutting—and you make him really important on that first step. He'll see that he's good at it and often he'll want to help others with it. But you have to watch for the next thing he can do. He's a normal human being and he'll get bored if he does nothing but saw, for instance. And if he gets bored, it's your fault, never the kid's fault. So he wants to know how to do a second thing, maybe drill the holes in the parts where the joints are. If you're really aware, then you've got him. You make him a magician at it.

"It's like Remigio, who didn't want to paint any colors. The minute he became the magician who could make green, his eyes were popping and he was becoming more and more a real, capable person. After green, he wanted to make purple, to make orange. Then we made a color chart and he was ready to do the mixing, to understand the magic of color. That was my job, to see what was missing in him and to expose him to something greater, a bigger world. And if you miss that moment of opportunity, you can lose the kid for good.

"That kind of observing can't take place when you have thirty kids in a group. There's no way you can work with more than four, maybe six, at a time. And if you can see their potential, all the better. I think that's what I'm good at now, after all these years, seeing which ones have the potential not just to produce but to pass their knowledge on to other kids down the line. If you can capture four or five children like that, then maybe each one can teach another one. You have to see the project that way because you won't be there forever. You have to see the project not just for what it is today, but how you want it to be in two or three years.

"After about three years, some of these kids can really make toys and teach others how to as well. Maybe they get really good at four or five toys. Let them be absolutely efficient at making those. Maybe it's not all the toys I'd like to see them make, but let them do what they want to do and if they want to add another one, it's up to them. I think it's much better than bombarding them with everything at once, expecting them to produce right away."

Hanni always starts the children off by making the bird, in memory of her pet bird Mimi, who died. It's a very simple, three-part toy: two wings and a body. By pulling strings attached to the wings, the child suddenly brings the bird to life.

"This is such a good toy to start with," Hanni says, "because it's so simple. But it teaches left and right—that's the message of the left and right wings, because when they're painted wrong, you have one backwards. The kids get so embarrassed about making that mistake! They learn to measure, how to cut and sand and paint. And the bird moves. A child who has said, 'I can't do that' suddenly says, 'Wow! I really did it!' Even very disabled children can make the bird."

There are other things Hanni has taught the children as well. About traditional toys that are in danger of dying out, for one. The acrobat, or *maro-mero*, the figure on strings between two sticks of wood who flips over when the sticks are squeezed together, has disappeared in many places. But the fathers and grandfathers remember with pleasure this simple toy that Hanni has brought back into many families. When there was only the macho male acrobat—*El gordo*, the Fat Man, Hanni calls him—she invented the gorgeous lady Mara and an iguana, an animal familiar to Mexican children, this one with chicken pox. And again, Mimi the bird.

One of everybody's favorite toys is Frida Kahlo. Until Hanni came into their lives, none of the children had ever heard of one of Mexico's most important twentieth-century artists. An influential painter and innovator in her own right, Frida was sometimes overshadowed by her famous husband, Diego Rivera, but she is now recognized for the imagination and beauty of her work and her influence on other artists. An independent and colorful spirit, like Hanni herself, with whom she has much in common (including being a disabled person), Frida now joyfully rides a rooster with bobbing head, legs, and tail. Her heavy eyebrows and the wildly colorful clothes the children give her—along with "Viva Frida" sometimes painted on the rooster's side—identify her immediately. And the children have learned something of their own heritage. "It's not just teaching the toy," Hanni says. "You can teach something else, too, using the toy as a tool."

Hanni's not as strong these days as she once was, and when she's asked, as she often is, to start another workshop, she wishes for a book like this one and maybe a video so that others can take advantage of her experience.

"I know there are places all over the world for projects like this one: rehabilitation centers, hospitals, community centers, schools. Even parents who just want to do something fun and creative with their kids can get involved.

"People think, 'Oh, but there's no money in it.' Of course there's no money in it! That's not what it's about. I couldn't do it if money were involved and I had to rely on money. I do this as a volunteer and my payment is seeing kids who get to realize that they are somebody. And a lot of them will produce something fantastic—they're really, truly artists."

Some lucky people even get to be clear about their purpose in life. The government of Ontario was clear about the importance of Hanni's work when they awarded her a medal for good citizenship, and in 2001 she was awarded Canada's prestigious Meritorious Service Medal, for teaching children to make toys.

Chapter 2

The Toy Workshop

Many readers of this book will want to establish toy-making workshops for the groups they serve. For them, we offer the workshop wisdom Hanni accumulated over the years, followed by instructions and patterns for twelve of her toys.

Other readers may simply want to have the fun of making Hanni's toys for themselves, their families, or friends. For these readers, instructions and patterns begin on page 39.

To all our readers: Enjoy!

Workshop Goals and How to Get There

The goal is more than simply to set up situations in which people can produce toys that may be charming or even profitable. It is something bigger: qualitative change in many lives. We all share a lifelong need for nurturing, so fostering development of the best we can be should be a fundamental concern of every group we belong to, from family and friends to government at every level.

You will find that the focus and the language used here are, for the sake of simplicity, directed to toy-making workshops for disabled and/or disadvantaged people, but this handbook is meant for people of both genders, all ages, and all levels of ability. No one is excluded, for what we're really talking about is promoting human growth and empowerment. And there may be shifts back and forth between "him" and "his" and "her" and "hers," but both genders are always intended.

Here are the goals:

- To give dignity and identity to slow learners, the disadvantaged, all people—in their own estimation and that of others—as useful, creative human beings.

- To promote the integration of able and disabled people within a healthy, functioning community.
- To encourage reasonable risk taking—important in the lives of all of us—in individuals who are often overprotected.
- To develop the full potential of people at a disadvantage to become artists, teachers, and leaders.
- To open an avenue to financial self-sufficiency for economically marginal people. (You're right, the profit motive lurks here, too, but you can see that it's at the bottom of the list.)

Here are some ideas that will be of value to you as you embark on a remarkable adventure:

- It's not necessary to be a trained teacher in order to be an effective project leader or coordinator, but some characteristics are essential:

A love of toys and play

Patience in abundance

Powers of observation

Imagination and the capacity to consider alternative approaches

Openness to the opinions of others

Belief in the possible

- Assumptions are useful, but only up to a point; we all use them and sometimes to our disadvantage. Be prepared to look for the ones that hold up and drop the ones that don't.
- Never underestimate a workshop participant's ability to perform, to create, and to express herself, no matter what her mental or physical disability. There are untapped capacities and subterranean rivers of humanity and individuality to be discovered. You will be astounded, often, at what comes to the surface.
- Be ready to share authority and release responsibility to your workshop participants. Remember, your aim is to empower and, not incidentally, to train teachers and coordinators who can carry on after

you leave the project. This means involving the group in all aspects of project operation and decision making.

- All individuals, groups, and communities have their own unique needs and desires. Be an anthropologist and make sure you understand those about you.
- Remember, if it's not fun, your participants will leave you. Let them feel your excitement and delight and don't be a heavy-handed overseer. Reluctance on the part of some to join in will melt away when they see what a good time you're having making toys—even if you have to do it by yourself for a while.
- Use your imagination to find ways to include everyone. The blind can sand and paint primer coats, the one-armed can drill holes.
- Everyone in the project—you as well as your participants—will make mistakes from time to time. Expect them, and expect to learn from them.
- Document your participants' progress. Make photographs if you can and, if you can't, make note of when they started work and when their first functioning toy was completed. They'll be amazed and take great pride in their accomplishment.
- Quality of the toys may—will—vary, but encourage the highest standards participants can reasonably be expected to meet. Quality means hard work, but if toys don't function and aren't attractively painted, for example, they won't satisfy their makers and they won't sell.

Everyone's circumstances will be different in the details of participants, location, funding available, and so on, but you'll find here the most important points you need to consider as you establish what may turn out to be one of your most rewarding projects ever. Now, let's get started.

Where to Begin

Actually, as far as physical space requirements go, you can start a toy-making project just about anywhere, from a well-equipped woodworking or crafts shop to a shed with interested participants, a table, chairs, and enough light to see what you're doing.

All but one of the Oaxaca workshops were started at the invitation of an existing organization: a school, a rehabilitation center for disabled children, a community center providing structured opportunities for all ages, and an education center for street children. The fifth project was begun at the invitation of an ad hoc community group that saw what had been accomplished by an earlier project.

It is important to have a connection with an existing group, for they will be helpful in providing the space and materials you need, finding helpers, and ensuring continuity when you are no longer part of the project. Seek ways, however, to keep your connection with the cooperating or sponsoring organization loose enough so that you don't get caught up in the time-consuming demands of a bureaucracy.

The places in the world appropriate for a toy-making workshop are almost limitless, for the pleasures and benefits of making toys are universal. Because of the developmental possibilities of toy making, natural centers are hospitals, rehabilitation centers, long-term care facilities, schools and centers for the disabled and disadvantaged, boys' and girls' clubs, and centers for community and enterprise development. Not to be neglected, however, are all the places where "normal" adults and children gather to work and play.

The space and equipment can be minimal. A list of necessary tools and other items follows. Again, use your imagination. Remember the project started in an area so poor they couldn't afford paintbrushes? Did they give up? No, they used sticks with dog hair. That's ingenuity!

Tools and Materials

Following are the items needed for a group of ten to forty children or adults. Keep in mind, however, that large groups should be broken into smaller ones and should have no more than four to six children or eight adults, possibly fewer, depending on their characteristics and special needs. Some participants will require one-on-one instruction.

If electricity and money are available:
2 scroll saws
1 drill press (If electricity is not available, use manual saws and drills.)

You also will need:

- 1 to 3 pairs of needle-nose pliers
- 1 to 3 hammers, sized to fit the hands that will be using them
- 1 to 3 screwdrivers
- 2 to 5 pairs of inexpensive scissors (not plastic, which break easily)
- Screws and carpet tacks with flat heads
- Copper wire
- Carpenter's glue
- Lightweight nylon fishing line
- Elastic thread (for the cowboy toy only)
- Multicolored, fine nylon cord for operating toys (strong string can be used if cord is unavailable)
- Fine and medium sandpaper (all children, regardless of disability, should use regular sandpaper, not hand sanders)
- 1 small, 1 medium, and 1 large paintbrush for each participant
- Durable paper for patterns (brown wrapping paper is good)
- ⅛" (3 mm) and 3⁄16" (5 mm) wood (scrap wood sawed into thin slices or old vegetable-crate wood will work fine; often this wood will be donated)
- Water-based acrylic paint in the primary colors, red, yellow, and blue, plus black and white (you can add more colors later)
- Nontoxic water-based varnish (some paints don't require varnish)
- Shoe box for each participant to contain work in progress

Staffing

The number of helpers you need will depend, of course, on the number and nature of your participants. If you have a group as large as forty children or adults, you'll probably need at least two or three assistants.

The necessary characteristics of leaders/teachers already mentioned bear repeating. They must have a real love of toys and a deep commitment to the project. They need enormous patience, the capacity to keep the enterprise fun, and a willingness to serve as examples. They must pay attention to detail but stop short of perfectionism. They mustn't mind getting their hands dirty when necessary: gardens grow with soil, seeds, and water, not lectures on horticulture.

Trained social workers and teachers can be wonderful instructors. Remember, though, that they cost money that often could be better spent on more materials for the workshop. So in addition to the professional help you can afford to hire, watch your participants for particularly talented and interested artists, no matter how young or old. They can be shown how to become leaders and assume the responsibility it's your aim to develop. Some of them will provide continuity for the project when you leave.

Find the coordinators in the community—mothers, fathers, uncles, and aunts. They understand their children and neighbors and have a special commitment to the workshop. Pay them for their work; they won't cost as much as professionals, and they'll do a good job for you.

Realize, too, that as your toy makers develop, they can take on such responsibilities as tracking what materials are running low and seeing that equipment is kept clean and in place. Rather than being a burden, these tasks can be seen as emblems of ownership in the project.

Invite outsiders with fresh ideas to come in from time to time. Their participation can be wonderfully stimulating to everybody.

If you're lucky enough to have volunteers, be sure they'll be around long enough to learn the job and develop a real commitment to the people they're working with. Some volunteers like to contribute money as well as time.

Family and Community Involvement

It's important that families and the community understand and support the purposes and the products of your project. In some cases, children will be returning to their families. In others, family involvement can even lead to toy making on a family basis, producing enough income to prevent flight to the city in search of nonexistent work.

A good way to include the community is to hold open houses, monthly if possible, when participants can be seen at work. Don't be discouraged if only a few people show up at first. People talk and their curiosity will draw them in. Once there, they will be amazed, delighted, and filled with pride at the accomplishments they see.

Promote family and community involvement at their pace, not yours. Some communities are suspicious of strangers and need to be shown that your intentions are good and that their children are benefiting from your work with them. Ultimately, they will understand that you care about them all and are a part of them. Family members and the larger community can be wonderful sources of ideas, materials, and psychological support. Invite them in.

Funding

Financial support is not an easy issue. Few projects find funds flowing to them without effort. Most foundations will not entertain grant requests from individuals, so it's necessary to establish a connection with a recognized nonprofit organization. When you have done this, learn how to write a good grant proposal, keeping your requests specific and reasonable. Good books on the topic can be very helpful.

If you are working in a foreign country, see whether your country's embassy has funds for assistance there. The Canadian embassy in Mexico, for example, was most generous in donating workshop equipment to two Oaxaca projects.

Inquire about funding from both governmental and nongovernmental agencies whose work could involve a toy-making project. Talk to the hospitals, rehabilitation centers, schools, and community centers in your area.

Be aware that funders will not be prepared to underwrite your activities forever, so look to ways in which you can become self-sustaining as soon as possible.

Most important, remember that a toy-making project will never be a big money maker—unless you're exploiting your participants. Your rewards will come primarily from the meaningful changes you have been able to bring about in others' lives.

Pricing and Selling the Toys

You'll have to feel your way on pricing; it will vary from area to area. Keep prices reasonable in relation to other toys available in your market region and then see how sales go.

There are several ways the toys can be sold. First, depending on location, the toy maker can sell directly to the client, keeping for himself all but a nominal amount to be turned back to the workshop for materials. For example, at Piña Palmera, in Mexico, the children were able to sell their products directly to tourists on the beach.

Second, the toy maker can get someone else to sell the toys for her and pay that person a commission. (The toy makers at Piña Palmera hated giving up any of their profit to an agent!)

Third, where markets are distant or participants are unable to go out and sell on their own, the collected toys can be taken to outlets such as folk-art stores, toy shops, museum shops, and hotel gift shops where tourists congregate. The workshop participants agree on an asking price and then divide the proceeds equally. When dealing with outlets, insist, if you can, on outright purchase of the toys, not a consignment arrangement.

The first two of these selling methods are really the best because they reinforce the toy makers' understanding of the need for quality, teach them sales skills, and make them aware of the pleasure of doing something well. Responsibility will develop naturally and they will be farther along the road to self-sufficiency.

Since you're not running a toy factory, it's often difficult to keep toy production at a constant level for the outlets you develop. Keep in mind that a well-made, handcrafted object has a charm and value no machine-produced item can ever have. Success in selling, however, will encourage participants to produce their wares on a reasonably consistent basis.

Accounting

Accounts can be simple, but they must be kept with regularity in order to avoid chaos and the possible misdirection of funds. The most important items to be tracked are the cost of materials, payment received, and distribution of profits.

Keep your eyes open for a participant who can be trained to take over the task of bookkeeping, with supervision at first. It will relieve you of a burden and enhance that person's self-esteem to be considered up to such an important job.

Recognize that accounting—and your operation in general—will necessarily be more complex if you're working with the help of a grant.

Assessing the Success of the Project

In assessing the success of a project such as this, it's possible to count businesses established and individuals who have become financially self-sufficient. Both are important measures of accomplishment. However, the most important outcomes you've been working toward have no financial value. They are self-esteem where little or none may have existed before; a capacity to undertake risk and responsibility; and a broader understanding of the underlying creativity, individuality, and potential of all people. (Remember the stories of Tino, Carlos, Isaías and Élida, and Jorge.) These measures of success will be apparent to everyone and constitute the most meaningful bottom line of all.

Leaving the Workshop

Ultimately, the day will come when you have to leave the workshop. If you have done your work well, you will have trained others to continue the work, following your guidelines but also incorporating their own innovations and improvements. Some of the people you leave behind may be professional teachers or social workers. Probably the most committed inheritors of your role, however, will come from among those for whose benefit you began the workshop in the first place or those members of the community you took on as paid nonprofessionals. These are the people who have the deepest commitment to seeing the project's work continue, for they understand its importance from the ground up. They are now teachers and leaders and should be recognized and paid accordingly.

Be pleased that you can leave your dedicated work in such hands. And don't be surprised to find changes when you come back to visit in a year's time or more. After all, you've achieved what you set about to establish: an entity of value that grows and changes, as all living things do.

Guiding Principles for Workshop Management

As your workshop evolves, so will the underlying principles along which you run it. Here are some of the fundamentals that have become clear over the years as the toy-making workshops in Mexico were established. They may prove helpful to you.

No one has to be excluded. Even the apparently most disabled who wish to join the group can and should be encouraged to do so. It's tempting to go by an accepted diagnosis and to assume limits that may well not exist—to deny the miracle of the possible. Patience, close observation, and creativity on your part will surely be required to discover the means by which such people can work, but there will be enormous rewards for everyone when a breakthrough comes. In settings where participants are—to the naked eye—without disabilities, see whether there are slow learners who can be encouraged to join in. The learning that will take place all around will be gratifying.

Your participants have special characteristics. Know them and work accordingly. For example, because of the demands of day-to-day survival, street children frequently have great difficulty in concentrating and are likely to be unruly. The physically immobilized, on the other hand, often have great powers of concentration, for they are called upon to think about every movement they make. In addition, their history of limitations usually produces eager learners.

Be sensitive, too, to the circumstances from which participants come. Many children in impoverished areas are obliged to contribute to the family's support and haven't the luxury of taking part in the fun of toy making. Respect that need and talk with parents to see whether there are ways in which their children can participate.

Progress and expectations need pacing. In their eagerness to make a finished toy, many children want to slight the necessary steps to produce a working toy. Slow them down, but also let them make mistakes. They'll quickly learn that it's less work in the long run to do it right from the beginning and that repairs are tedious. Encourage them in what they're good at, like cutting or sanding, and acknowledge those new skills. Make them feel important and then let them move on. Pace them so that they don't become bored.

Disruptive members can be brought around. Occasionally, a child or young person will disrupt the work of the group. Often, the group itself will demand cooperation and orderly behavior, even to the point of excluding the troublemaker. If that doesn't happen, don't be afraid to preserve a peaceful working environment for the rest. Don't be afraid to make it clear that disrupters will be asked to leave. They will probably return, because no one likes to be left out of the fun.

Responsibility is a gift. Too often people with disabilities are overprotected and denied the opportunity to become truly responsible, contributing members of society. Let them be all they can be. Just go slowly, from Step A to Step B to Step C.

Application is a great way to learn. Every part of the toy-making process has some useful fallout. For example, no one can make a workable toy without learning how to measure—practicing some arithmetic, that is. Others will improve their reading and writing skills as they become entrepreneurs on a modest scale, keep accounts, and become successful marketers of their products. The visible utility of these skills is a wonderful motivator.

The best toys come from what their makers know. Every culture has rich traditions that deserve to be kept alive in one form or another. To set out to manufacture copies of already mass-produced artifacts can only stifle individuality and creativity, and such products will have little sales appeal. Here are opportunities to teach about a culture's greatness, about its heroes, about its rich resources. Encourage fantasy and variation on such themes, and you'll be delighted with what results.

Learning how to make a toy is fun and, without realizing it, children learn measuring, math, writing, and some science. They can also become truly creative artists, significantly enhancing the quality of their lives.

The Bird   Page 42

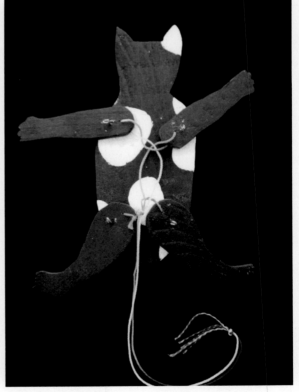

The Cat   Page 44

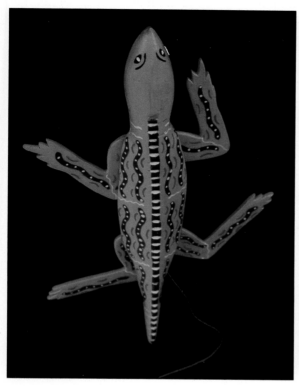
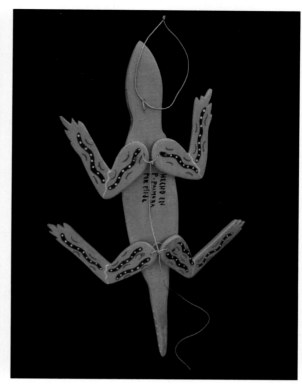

The Crocodile

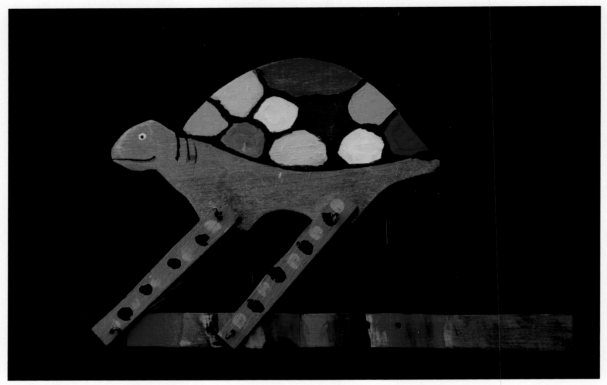

The Turtle

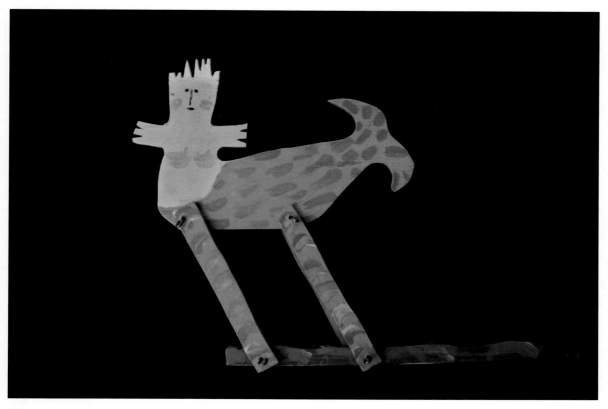

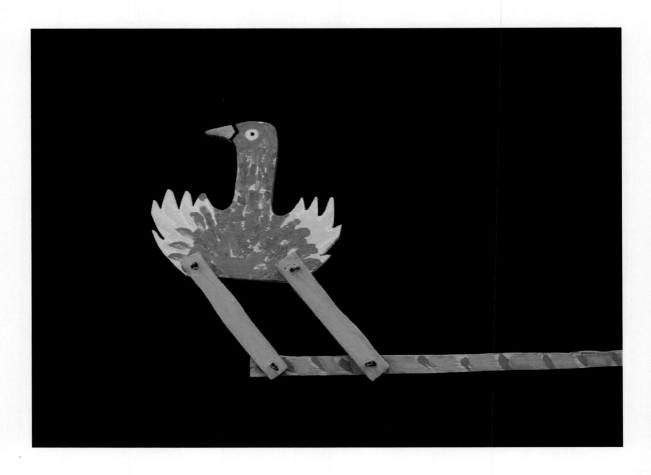

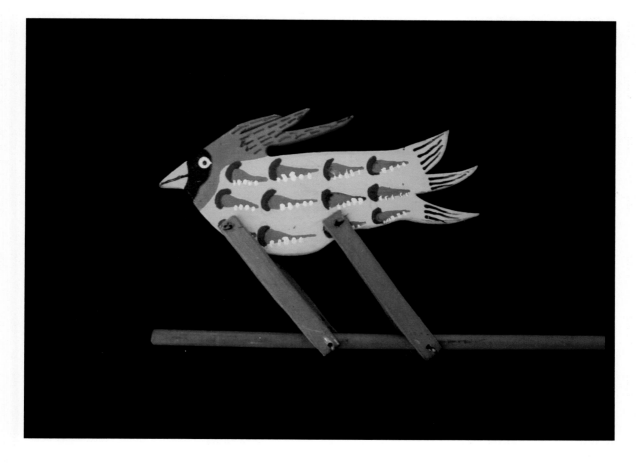

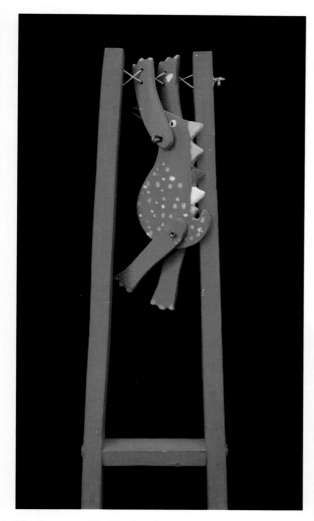

The Iguana with Chicken Pox   Page 52

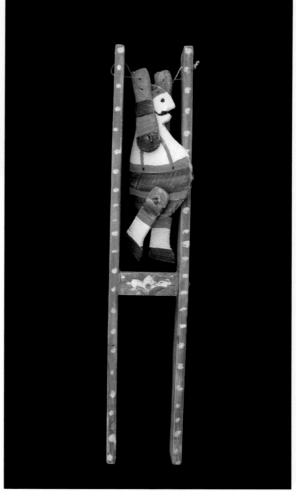

The Fat Man   Page 55

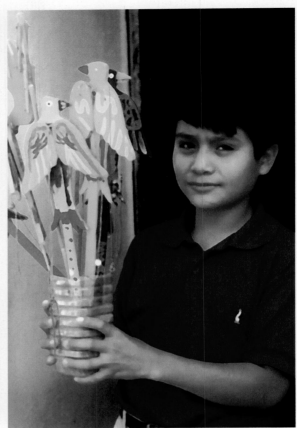

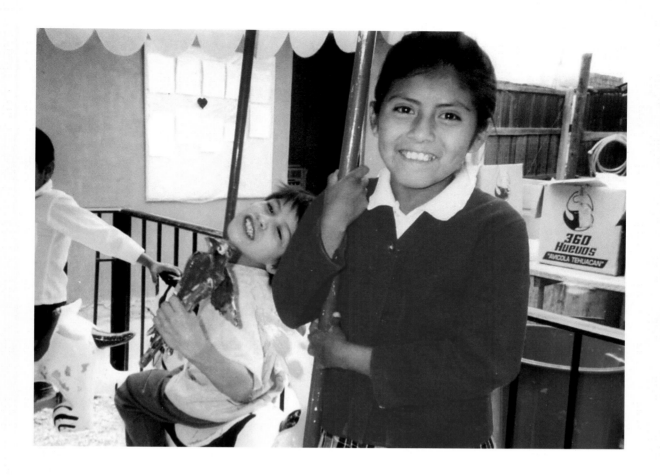

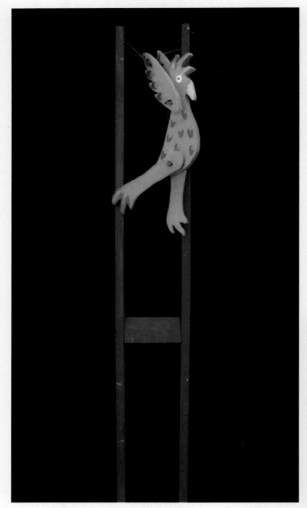

Mimi   Page 55

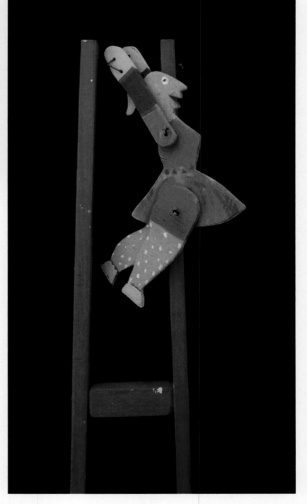

Mara   Page 57

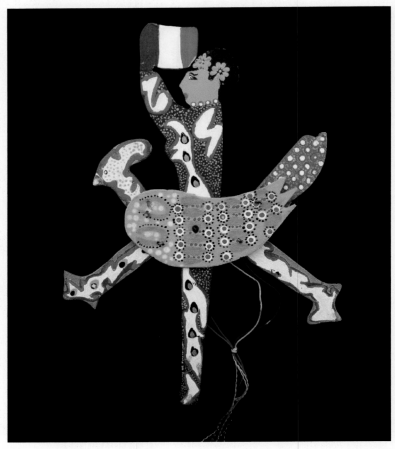

Viva Frida

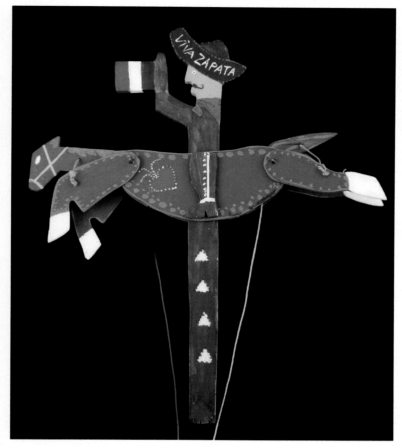

Viva Zapata   Page 62

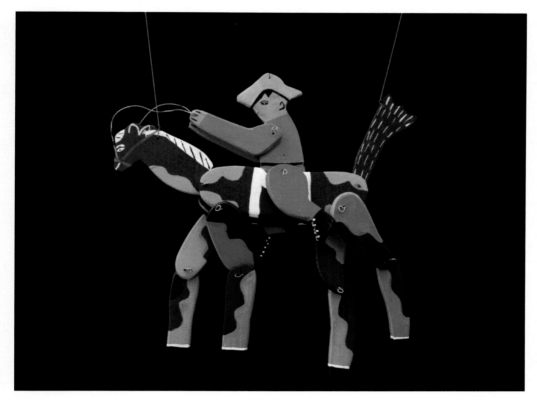

The Cowboy   Page 64

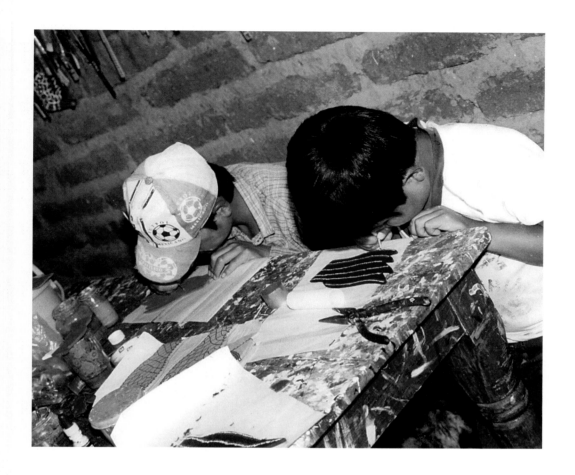

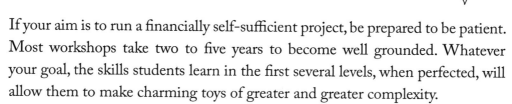

Chapter 3

Instructions and Patterns

If your aim is to run a financially self-sufficient project, be prepared to be patient. Most workshops take two to five years to become well grounded. Whatever your goal, the skills students learn in the first several levels, when perfected, will allow them to make charming toys of greater and greater complexity.

The teacher is always the first student, so make at least one example of each toy yourself before you attempt to teach others.

Note that patterns have not been included for some toy variations (the Crocodile, for example, which is made like the Cat). Also, for ease in photocopying or tracing, the patterns have been drawn with heavy lines. We recommend that you not cut the patterns out of the book—pieces are likely to get lost, and you'll also lose the instructions on the next page.

Level 1

The first-level toys are the Bird and its variations, the Cat and the Crocodile, and two stick toys, the Turtle and the Mermaid. Next is the Iguana with Chicken Pox, a version of the *maromero,* a toy that flips over like an acrobat when the two sticks to which it's attached are squeezed together. The *maromero* can be made with endless variations, and here we give you three more: the Fat Man, Mara, and another Bird, Mimi.

In all the workshops, it has proved useful to start with the first Bird, a pull-string toy consisting of only three parts. It teaches all the skills you'll use again and again—cutting out the wooden parts, sanding them, drilling holes, assembling the parts correctly, and painting. (Remember, every bird has a left and a right wing!)

On the patterns, all holes marked "1" are for string or cord. All holes marked "2" are for copper wire. Before long, this consistent pattern will make assembly easy and automatic.

It's time now to get a shoe box or a container of similar size for each workshop participant. Each box, labeled with the student's name, will hold patterns, cut-out toy parts, and tools that don't have to be shared. If you're lucky enough to have paintbrushes to go around, they should be cleaned and kept here by each participant. Responsibility should begin at the beginning.

The Bird

Ask your students to make three birds. With the first, show them how. With the second, let them ask for help. With the third, let them struggle. They learn faster if they have to figure it out for themselves or, better, if they help each other. Once the bird is a success, they are eager to start on the second toy.

1. Have the students make a strong-paper pattern, tracing from the pattern provided here or from the bird parts you have made as a model.

2. Cut out the three parts, the two wings and the body, from $\frac{3}{16}$" (5 mm) wood.

3. Sand both sides of all the parts well.

4. Drill holes in the wings and body as indicated on the pattern.

5. Glue and nail a stick from an ice-cream bar or something similar to the back of the bird as a handle.

6. Apply the primer coat of paint, allow it to dry, and then have fun with bright colors and creativity. (All the toys that follow should receive a primer coat of paint as well.)

7. When the parts are dry, assemble them. First, pull a cord 16" (40 cm) long through hole 1 on each of the wings. Knot the cord near the wings, as indicated, leaving enough slack so that the wings can move.

8. To hold the body and wings together, insert copper wire through hole 2 on each wing and the body. Learn to make perfect loops on both ends of the wire with pliers. They should be small but firm so that they won't open.

9. Finish off the loose end of the cord nicely with a colorful bead or a small ball of clay. Pull the cord, and off your bird flies!

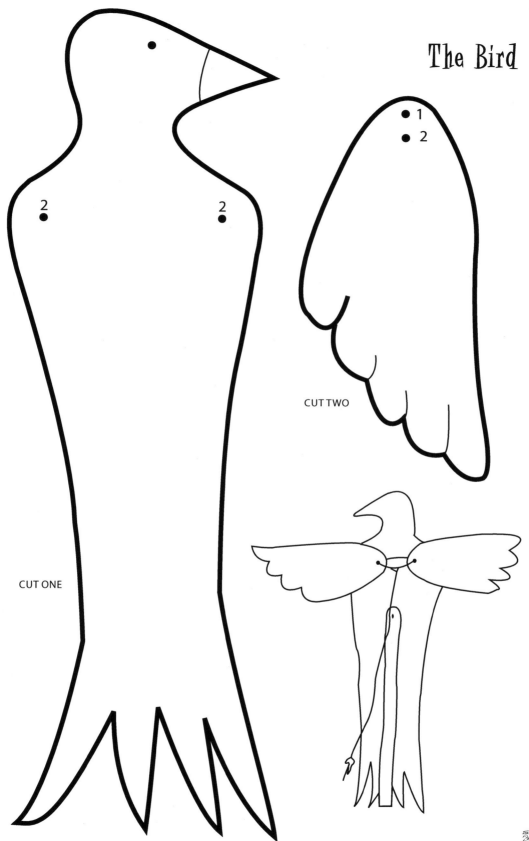

The Bird

CUT TWO

CUT ONE

The Cat

The Cat and the Crocodile (for which a pattern is not included) are made in the same way as the Bird, but they have four legs rather than two wings. A lot of variations can be made using this basic pattern.

The Cat

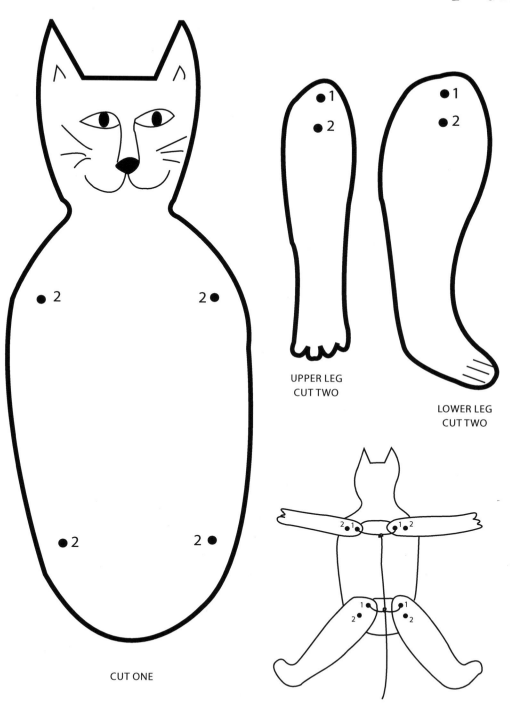

UPPER LEG
CUT TWO

LOWER LEG
CUT TWO

CUT ONE

The Turtle

The lesson here is to learn to measure perfectly. Seven-eighths of an inch is not an inch! At the toy workshop for the street kids in Oaxaca, most of the children had never seen a ruler. By the time they mastered the art of measuring, they measured everything in sight—arms, legs, noses!

This toy can represent any creature—the Turtle, the Mermaid, the Fat Cat—and variations are all made in the same way. It moves backward and forward by jiggling the stick on which it stands.

Each connector measures 2¾" × ⅜" (7 cm × 1 cm). The holes must measure the same distance apart on the stick as on the animal where the connectors are attached. If they don't, the toy won't flop down properly.

1. Cut the animal body from ³⁄₁₆" (5 mm) wood and the four connectors from ⅛" (3 mm) wood, ³⁄₁₆" (5 mm) wide and 2¾" (7 cm) long. Drill holes on the body *exactly* 2" (5 cm) apart.

2. Make a stick ⅜" × ⅜" by approximately 12" long (1 cm × 1 cm × 30 cm). Holes on the stick for attaching connectors should be exactly 2" (5 cm) apart and placed about 1" (2.5 cm) from one end of the stick, as shown. (Sticks of these dimensions can be found precut in some places; in others, natural materials, like *carrizo*, a plant similar to bamboo, can be used.)

3. Sand, paint, and assemble the pieces as you've already learned to do, using copper wire to fix the connectors to the body and sticks, but not too tightly so that the body can move back and forth.

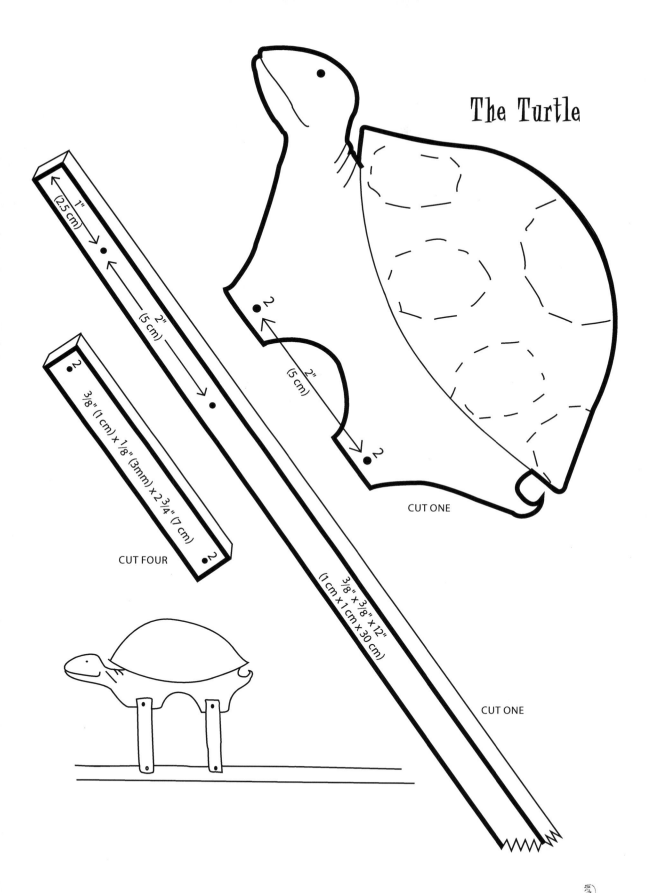

The Turtle

1"
(2.5 cm)

2"
(5 cm)

3/8" (1 cm) x 1/8" (3mm) x 2 3/4" (7 cm)

CUT FOUR

2

2"
(5 cm)

2

CUT ONE

3/8" x 3/8" x 12"
(1 cm x 1 cm x 30 cm)

CUT ONE

The Mermaid

CUT ONE

The Fat Cat

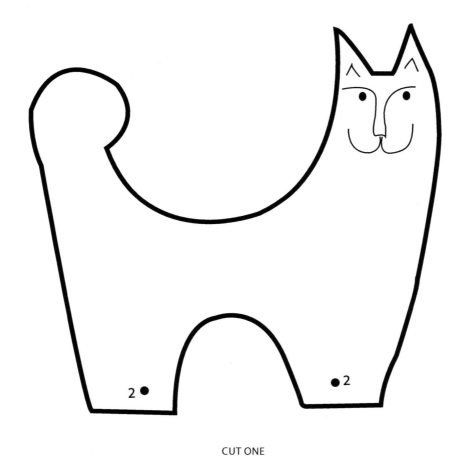

CUT ONE

The children now know how to measure, cut, sand, paint, and assemble a toy by themselves. Let them make these designs, plus the Bird, for several weeks until they feel truly self-confident.

The Iguana with Chicken Pox

The *maromero* has been with us for centuries, delighting millions of children and adults around the world. Making this toy teaches the importance of balance, weight, and gravity. If all parts of the toy are cut out and assembled correctly, you will have a creature that turns and dances endlessly when you squeeze the ends of the two sticks together.

The Fat Man, Mimi, and Mara are all are made in the same way as the Iguana with Chicken Pox. (Mara is a female because far too many traditional toys feature only males.)

1. Cut out all body parts from ⅛" (3 mm) wood.

2. Cut two sticks ⅜" × ⅜" × 12" (1 cm × 1 cm × 30 cm) long and a crossbar ⅜" × ⅜" × 2" (1 cm × 1 cm × 5 cm) long.

3. Sand and paint.

4. Assemble all the animal or figure parts with copper-wire loops.

5. Using small screws, join the two sticks and the crossbar 4" (10 cm) from the bottom of the sticks and 8" (20 cm) from the tops of the sticks.

6. Drill the top holes ¼" (7 mm) from the top of the sticks and the second ¼" (7 mm) below that.

7. Crisscross cord between the uprights and arms as shown.

8. Make strong double knots on the outside of the sticks to hold the cord firmly in place.

The Iguana with Chicken Pox

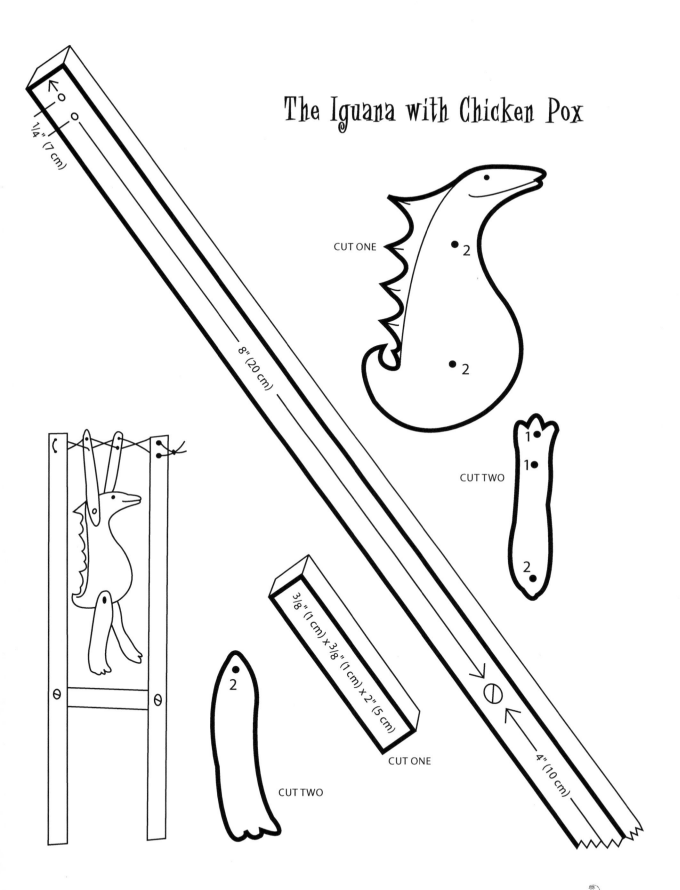

1/4" (7 cm)

8" (20 cm)

CUT ONE

2

2

1
1

CUT TWO

2

3/8" (1 cm) x 3/8" (1 cm) x 2" (5 cm)

CUT ONE

4" (10 cm)

2

CUT TWO

The Fat Man and Mimi

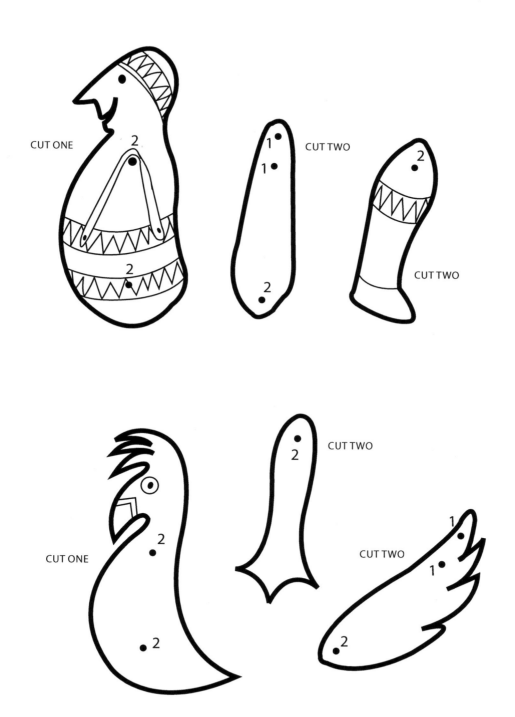

CUT ONE

CUT TWO

CUT TWO

CUT TWO

CUT ONE

CUT TWO

Instructions and Patterns **55**

Mara

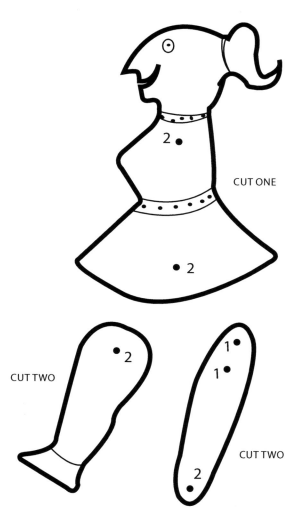

CUT ONE

CUT TWO

CUT TWO

After making these toys, the children should be self-confident enough to make their own variations of the acrobat.

Keep making these three designs, the Bird, the Turtle, and the Iguana with Chicken Pox and their variations for about a year, improving your work and learning from your mistakes. With encouragement, the children will be able to create beautiful, marketable toys.

Level 2

After producing a good, saleable toy at the first level, you can become more elaborate and make toys that have seven or more parts. These toys are more animated and must be measured accurately. At this stage, it's important to encourage the children to let their imaginations run free and to create their own designs. One year in Oaxaca, all the children's creatures—rabbits, iguanas, turtles—wore running shoes. One child had seen tourists wearing them and copied them with great delight.

Viva Frida

This toy is made in honor of Frida Kahlo, who had a great toy collection and has inspired many as a human being and artist. For many years, Frida, a disabled person, lived in the shadow of her husband, painter Diego Rivera. She has been recognized as a major, influential artist in her own right. Other culturally appropriate heroines and heroes can also be used.

1. Cut out the seven parts precisely. Frida's body and handle are ³⁄₁₆" (5 mm) wood and the remaining parts are ⅛" (3 mm) wood.

2. Sand and paint. Don't forget to emphasize Frida's heavy eyebrows and the flowers she so often wore in her hair. She should be gloriously decorative.

3. Drill holes as indicated.

4. Glue and tack one side of the bird's body to Frida and set it aside.

5. Attach cord 6" to 8" (15 cm to 20 cm) in length to the bird's two legs, head, and tail as indicated. Make double knots and secure them with a drop of glue. Remember, hole 1 is always for cord; hole 2 is always for wire.

6. Cut four pieces of copper wire 1¼" (3 cm) in length. Make a loop on one end of each piece of wire. Push the wire through the bird's body part that has been tacked to Frida, with the loops on the painted side of the body.

7. Now slide the head, tail, and legs that you have already attached cords to onto the wires sticking up from Frida.

8. Slide on the second half of the bird's body and tack it onto Frida as you did on the other side.

9. Finish the wire loops on the outer side of the bird's body.

10. Cut all cords to the same length. Tie their ends together and finish nicely with a bead or a clay ball at the end. Pull the strings and off she goes!

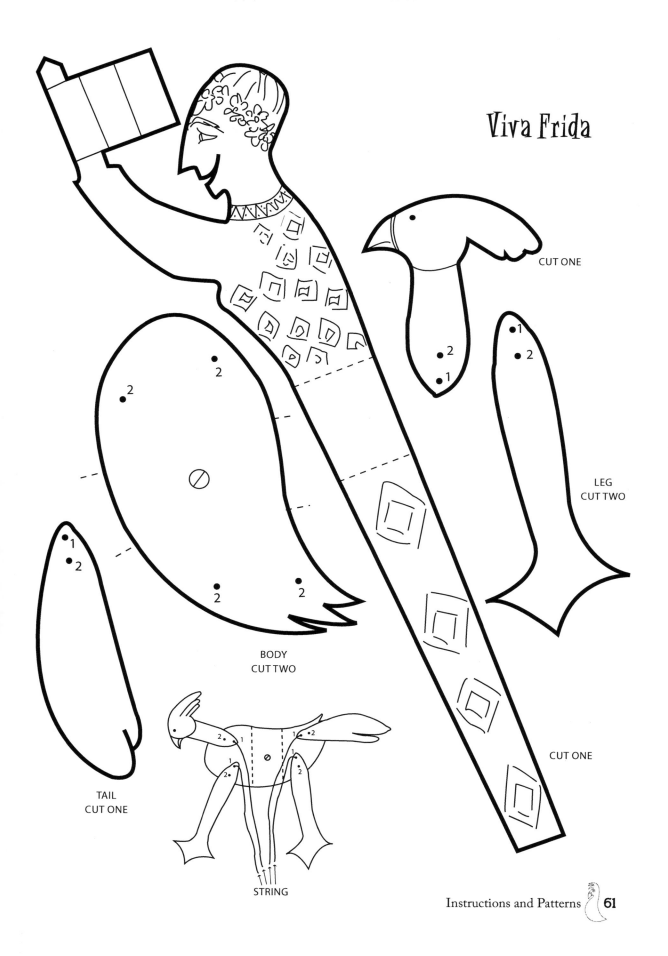

Viva Frida

CUT ONE

LEG
CUT TWO

CUT ONE

BODY
CUT TWO

TAIL
CUT ONE

STRING

Viva Zapata

Zapata is like Frida but consists of eleven parts. In this case, the head and tail are inside the horse's body, and the legs are outside. The body uses ³⁄₁₆" (5 mm) wood. The remaining parts are ⅛" (3 mm) wood. The boots are glued onto the horse last.

This toy is assembled in the same way as Frida except that the cord is also strung through the holes numbered 3 so that the head and tail raise both the front and back legs.

Both Frida and Zapata can be used to teach something about Mexican history. Every Mexican child knows about Emiliano Zapata, who was a peasant hero of the Mexican Revolution beginning in 1910, but few in the Oaxaca workshops had ever heard of Frida Kahlo. Every country has its heroes who should be celebrated.

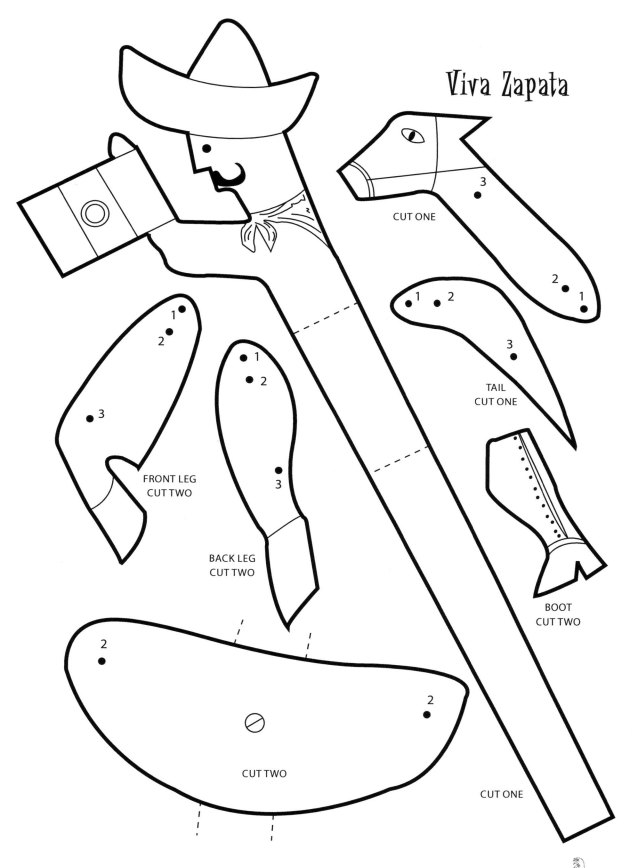

Viva Zapata

CUT ONE

TAIL
CUT ONE

FRONT LEG
CUT TWO

BACK LEG
CUT TWO

BOOT
CUT TWO

CUT TWO

CUT ONE

The Cowboy

This toy has seventeen parts. It's very elaborate and a great seller.

1. Cut the cowboy's body and the stick from which he hangs from ³⁄₁₆" (5 mm) wood. Make the stick 12" (30 cm) long. Cut the rest of the pieces from ⅛" (3 mm) wood.

2. Sand, paint, and assemble the parts as for Frida and Zapata.

3. Use an 8" (22 cm) piece of copper wire heavier than that used in the other toys to attach the cowboy's hand to the horse's head. If such wire is not available, you can use cord or string.

4. Cut a piece of string 16" (41 cm) long. Thread the string through the cowboy's head, then bring both ends through a hole in the center of the stick and make a firm knot.

5. Knot one end of a string approximately 11" (28.5 cm) and pull it through the hole marked 1 on the horse's tail. Pass the other end of the string through a hole near the end of the stick and secure it with a knot. Attach the horse's head and the stick in similar fashion.

6. Instead of attaching the horse's head and tail and the cowboy's head to the stick with plain cord, use elastic strings. The horse will jump in a much more realistic way.

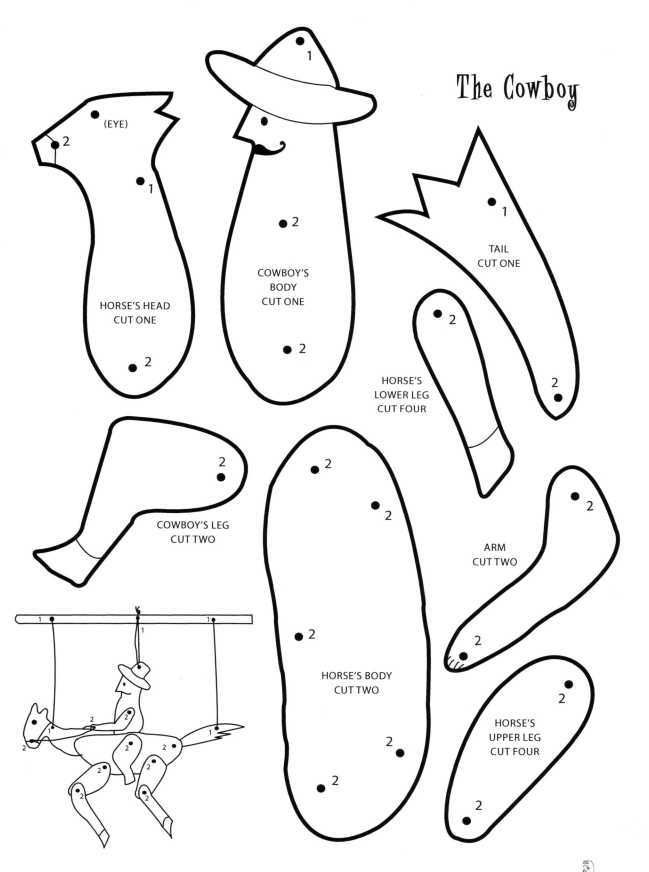

The Cowboy

1

(EYE)
2
1

HORSE'S HEAD
CUT ONE

1

2

COWBOY'S
BODY
CUT ONE

2

1

TAIL
CUT ONE

2

2

HORSE'S
LOWER LEG
CUT FOUR

2

2

COWBOY'S LEG
CUT TWO

2

2

2

ARM
CUT TWO

2

2

2

2

2

HORSE'S BODY
CUT TWO

2

2

2

HORSE'S
UPPER LEG
CUT FOUR

2

2

Looking Ahead

If your students are making these toys well and enjoying their work, you'll be having a great time. Now you know how much fun it is to make toys. You may be able, sometimes with a little help, to go on to make pull toys with wheels, toy cars, and so on. The possibilities are limitless.

If you've sold enough toys, it's now time to get more tools, such as an electric sander. Maybe you can afford (or can scavenge or obtain gratis) a band saw or the special part for the drill press that cuts wheels. All tools are investments to create better work. Perhaps at this point some organization will be so excited about your work that they would love to give you a grant. Ask!

Practice makes perfect. By the third level, most children and adults can go on making by themselves the toys for which patterns are provided.

The joy of seeing your well-made, creative toys (products) before you, or better, in a store or gallery, is overwhelming. As a teacher, you should be keeping your eyes open for the children and adults who may be the future teachers and leaders of your workshops. They will serve as wonderful examples to succeeding groups of toy makers and will love passing on their skills and experience.

The toy is a tool for creating communities that integrate all children and adults, both able and disabled. For some students, the toy becomes a new and meaningful mode of communication. But what you've found here is only the planting of the first seeds. Working with patience and imagination, you can provide nourishment for the young plants and develop self-confident human beings who take pride in themselves and, in some cases, may even become self-sufficient.

The toy takes us into a magic world we don't want to leave forever. It nourishes our senses, teaches us how to touch, feel, see, and love. And most important, it gives us a sense of security in our own personal world. Whether it's a teddy bear, a doll, a marble, even a blanket, our imaginations grow and take us wherever we want to go—fantasizing, imitating, creating, and learning.

The world has become my toy box. I play in it from the moment I wake up. Mind you, some days I play with the wrong toy, but I always learn and never stop playing.

—Hanni Sager